Dole queues and Industrial strife were omni-present in the Coventry of the 1980s

CORTICELLA

DiRTY STOP OUTS GUIDE TO 1980s Coventry

By Ruth Cherrington

Published by ACM Retro
www.acmretro.com

Other titles in this series:

Dirty Stop Out's Guide to 1970s Manchester.

Dirty Stop Out's Guide to 1970s Liverpool.

Dirty Stop Out's Guide to 1970s Coventry.

Dirty Stop Out's Guide to 1970s Barnsley.

Dirty Stop Out's Guide to 1950s Sheffield.

Dirty Stop Out's Guide to 1960s Sheffield.

Dirty Stop Out's Guide to 1970s Sheffield.

Dirty Stop Out's Guide to 1980s Sheffield.

Dirty Stop Out's Guide to 1990s Sheffield.

Dirty Stop Out's Guide to 1970s Chesterfield.

Dirty Stop Out's Guide to 1980s Chesterfield.

Dirty Stop Out's Guide to 1980s Chesterfield Quizbook.

We're on the look out for writers to cover other UK towns and cities
and we're always on the look out for great retro photos!
Please email us at **info@dirtystopouts.com** if you fancy getting involved.

www.dirtystopouts.com

Lifting the FA Cup brought the entire city together like never before

DiRTY STOP OUTS GUIDE TO 1980s Coventry

By Ruth Cherrington

DJ 'Rhythm Doc' Chris Long outside his clothes shop in Coventry with brother Simon and a friend. He says: "My clothes shop was formerly Le Brasseur which sold 'surgical appliances (plus sex aids under the counter!) I kept the old signage when I took it over. And just sold clothes!" (Photo: Marc Coker)

CONTENTS

Coventry's own King who enjoyed chart success in the latter half of the decade

COVENTRY ON THE DOLE SHOWS HOW TO DO TALENT AND TURNTABLES!

Aerial view of Coventry with Herbert Art Gallery and Odeon cinema

Who can forget the eerie whistling sound blowing through a bleak, deserted industrial town that led us into Ghost Town?

Spending three weeks at Number One in 1981, 2 Tone pioneers the Specials seemed to sum up what was happening to industrial cities like Coventry. It was named Single of the Year by all three top UK music magazines, but became much more than that - even an anthem for the decade.

Coventry was still making great music as the 1980s began, and great cars too, but clouds were on the horizon.

Sir Michael Edwardes, head of major local employer British Leyland, let loose a new year tirade against trade unionists and politicians who drove foreign cars: "They should buy British and save the home motor industry," accusing them of following an unpatriotic fashion.

Mike Lewis: "The 1980s was the era the city began to seriously lose its manufacturing base, but at the same time was creating a cultural identity by the people, for the people."

Local MP Leslie Huckfield added his gloomy warning that Coventry would soon become "Britain's industrial graveyard" if something wasn't done. A nice positive start to the decade, then!

Whilst the prospect of mass redundancies cast a shadow over the celebrations that greeted the new decade, the attitude of many was to have a good time while they still could!

Rob Summerfield: "The eighties! A great time for pubs and clubs in Coventry. It was a vibrant era for going out. I had lots of good times and some almighty hangovers."

View from Lower to Upper Precinct

Conflict was part of the backdrop, whether between young people and anyone over 25, political parties, workers and managers, feminist and sexists. Bands had their fair share of it as well. The Specials split in 1981, making Ghost Town the last single with that familiar line-up. Selecter members went their own ways as well. It seemed like the end of 2 Tone's reign.

But the music didn't die: this is Coventry we're talking about after all! If anything it ramped up several gears, showing that this gutsy city really had got talent. Plenty of home-grown musicians were notching up chart successes such as Hazel O'Connor, with successive hit singles from her Breaking Glass album, and a starring role in the film. The Reluctant Stereotypes, God's Toys, King and the Primitives added to Coventry's musical glory.

And the city's own independent radio station came on air in May 1980 - Mercia Sound. Broadcasting from a former Working Men's Club in Hertford Place, Mercia was enthusiastically welcomed by radio listeners bored with the same-old of the BBC.

The breakfast show Good Morning Mercia, with Gordon Astley, ran from 5am - 9.30am and was the background sound to many early morning cuppas, breakfasts and rush hours. Weather, news updates, music, traffic reports, competitions, jingles: Mercia had everything that listeners could want!

Ann Lucas: "Used to listen to Mercia sound every night until I fell asleep when I was in my teens. Missed it when I went to Plymouth to start University!"

Stuart Linnell was the voice of Afternoon Delight, on air between 1pm-4pm. Popular local DJ Jim Twyneham, known for his work with SILK disco, also joined the station.

It seemed that music-wise every man, woman and their dog wanted to show what they could do. And one man's dog did! Paxo stole the show during a gig his master Doc Mustard was doing with local band Hot Snacks.

"While we were performing at the Queens in Hillfields, Paxo calmly came on stage, crossed from left to right and departed on his merry way. The young rascal!"

Trev Teasdel reckons Paxo had just as much local fame as Doc Mustard himself!

Music was everywhere, from pub backrooms to the big venues, some of them with new names: Coventry Theatre became the Apollo, the Locarno, Tiffany's. Some musicians made the streets their stage such as busking duo Jimmy Jimmy, aka

Jimmy Kemp and James O'Neill. They even had a number one hit in Japan with I Met Her in Paris.

Coventry was exporting popular music but not enough cars - even though locals loved them. Colin Hughes was, and remains, a massive Triumph fan.

"My first car was a Triumph as were I think the next eight! My dad worked in the Triumph factory and had one too as did our neighbours."

Arnold William: "Cars are just in our blood in Coventry as well as in many pub names!"

Col Hughes' 1982 Triumph

Triumph family! Col Hughes and his dad show off their cars, 1983

Local loyalty could only save a small part of Coventry's manufacturing industry. No wonder that Ghost Town struck such a chord. It probably wasn't heard in Downing Street where Mrs. Thatcher was top of the political pops. The UK's first female PM was hell-bent on making her own mark on the country, whether we wanted it or not. She claimed she had engineered a 'loadsamoney' economy. But for many, it was redundancy or dole money.

Those with little more than a UB40 in their final wage packet weren't laughing all the way to the bank, unlike the recently created 'yuppies' – the catch all term for anyone affluent and the right

Production halved at BL car factories

PUTTING THE BIG MOMENT ON RECORD

o longer needed after plant take-over
500 JAGUAR MEN LOSE CITY JOBS

side of 30 in the era. But laugh we did, at comedian Harry Enfield's obnoxious, foul mouthed 'loadsamoney' character who we loved to hate. The single he made with the same name in April 1988 went into the charts at Number Four.

Trev Teasdel: *"Spitting Images with the revolving head of Thatcher, turning but not turning!"*

Spitting Image puppets of politicians and celebrities hit our screens in 1984, providing entertainment and a small form of revenge. Not even the Royal Family was immune from their special form of lampooning. Mrs Thatcher, the Iron Lady, was the constant backdrop of the decade, both in real life and comedy images.

Alternative comedy, cafés, co-ops and collectives were so common they became the mainstream. Even musicians and DJs formed collectives, so committed were they to keeping the turntables revolving and the good times rolling.

The Wedge café in the High Street became campaign central, serving up coffees and community action. Many people were so busy campaigning that they made a career out of it. Revolution was in the air as we donned berets, pulled on big boots and headed for the next demo.

Worrying head-lines for British Leyland workers

There was plenty to protest against, with high unemployment, US missiles coming to Greenham Common, war with Argentina, a cold one with the USSR, Mrs. T's one with the 'enemy within,' the closure of coal mines, racist attacks, education cuts and more.

Gill Dawson: *"This was a decade when I got involved in politics. Standing on the steps of the Lanch student union wearing my charity shop mac, docs and a beret (very Citizen Smith!) collecting money for the miners."*

Some young people's discontent went beyond demos, erupting into rioting and fighting rival groups. Some young people just put on their skates instead as roller discos came to town. In the 1980s Jules Little was "a ginger kid who loved music, girls, roller skating, not always in that order." He ended

Photographer Bill Boswell looks at the city from a different angle- from under the Ring Road!

Right: Bill Boswell captures people enjoying the spring blossoms in the Precinct

Punks gathering outside Fosters in Broadgate

up as a DJ. There was fun to be had, after all and Jules was not the only one finding it.

Nick Edgington really liked Coventry in the 1980s. He gave up trying to be a student and got himself a job at the GEC. A career in buying followed and meant Nick could do some spending.

"I went to plenty of gigs at the Lanch, General Wolfe, Coventry Theatre/ Apollo, Tiffany's and other local venues."

For Tracey McAtamney, 1985 was "a year to remember!" As a glamorous Carnival Queen, she was treated like royalty while fulfilling her duties. It wasn't all posh lunches and trips to

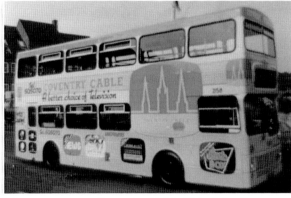

Who remembers Coventry Cable Television?

Coventry cathedrals old and new

the hairdressers: Tracey worked hard to raise thousands for local charities.

Whilst some of the changes the eighties brought were far from welcome, we got them anyway, along with things we really took to. The Sony Walkman, forerunner of the iPod 20 years later, enabled us to listen to music as we jogged, ate and just about everything else. Amstrad computers seemed very high tech, the first really affordable home computers.

Channel 4 came on air in November 1982 with a remit to cater more for minority tastes. Some said it had no taste at all with too much breaking down the boundary of decency. Plenty of swearing and sex then! And lots of 'yoof' programmes, such as The Tube, with its 'shock horror' factor.

Coventry kept up with the trends with its own local cable TV channel-COLT. Gillian Dawson remembers its Not by Satellite programme and a 'brilliant' video of local band the Giraffes. Guitarist in the band Nigel Williams remembers that very well. Steve Ashwell was involved in this innovative projects and talks of its community-based focus.

Coventry also took a big interest in the wider world and often showed its big heart. The city rallied behind Live Aid in 1985 and staged its own version, CovAid, to raise money for famine relief. Local bands rushed to offer their help and fans rushed to buy tickets.

Coventry band TDA playing at CND rally 1982

The decade was packed with some of the old plus a lot of new as well. Punks could be found in the city centre. Rockers frequented pubs like the 'Dive' while flamboyant, floppy haired fashionistas were spotted in others. Big hair, shoulder pads, power dressing and dodgy perms all vied for our attention.

Rich Mulligan: "The regular meet up place for punks for a good while was 'the benches' outside WH Smiths, often before heading to a gig at the Brewer, Hand and Heart, or the Stoker."

Photographer Robin Brooker captures workmen in action rebuilding historic Spon Street

For Sid Wilson, some of the decade was spent at school, some of it getting drunk. "Not while at school, obviously!" He did a fair bit of collecting vinyl and going to gigs.

Sue Lowe: "Perms, frosted highlights. Hair was huge!"

Belts were tightened all round but people still liked the occasional gastronomic treat. They headed into town to eat at their favourite restaurants, such as the Rajah. Colin Horton's love of curry was nurtured there and even led to his first marriage.

And whilst on the subject of eating, 1980 gave Coventry cinemas our first sighting of a very nasty 'thing' bursting out of John Hurt's chest, right in the middle of dinner! Little did we know that we'd be seeing a lot more of that thoroughly unpleasant creature, with Ridley Scott's Alien the first of many.

A musical great was lost to us with the murder of John Lennon in New York on December 8th 1980. It was the day that local musician Martin Bowes first performed with his band Attrition. Perhaps not a good omen at the time but they're still going strong.

"TOO MUCH TOO YOUNG (LIVE EP)"
SPECIAL AKA
NUMBER 1 IN 1980

"RAT RACE/RUDE BOYS OUTA JAIL"
THE SPECIALS
NUMBER 5 IN 1980

"EIGHTH DAY"
HAZEL O'CONNOR
NUMBER 5 IN 1980

"STEREOTYPE/INTERNATIONAL JET
THE SPECIALS
NUMBER 6 IN 1980

Local band the Attrition of Reason promo shot 1984

Martin Bowes and Attrition live at the Queen's Inn, Hillfields, 1981

Later in the decade Coventry's football team the Sky Blues raised everyone's spirits when they lifted the FA Cup on May 16th 1987. Coventry City were the underdogs against Tottenham and the possibility of them winning was scoffed at by the pundits.

But the whole of Coventry cheered loudly and for a very, very long time, in their "sky blue heaven" after the famous 3-2 victory. It was a moment many will never forget and is etched onto the city's collective memory forever. It was a wonderful tonic in a creatively vibrant, musically buzzing yet economically challenging decade.

Welcome to 1980s Coventry!

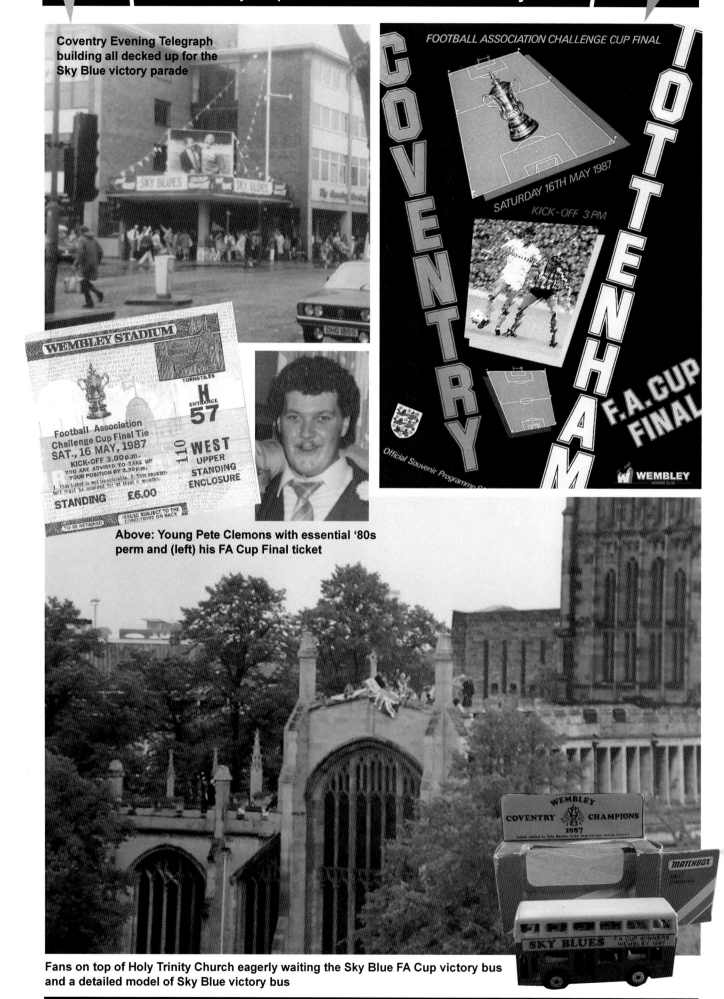

Coventry Evening Telegraph building all decked up for the Sky Blue victory parade

Above: Young Pete Clemons with essential '80s perm and (left) his FA Cup Final ticket

Fans on top of Holy Trinity Church eagerly waiting the Sky Blue FA Cup victory bus and a detailed model of Sky Blue victory bus

SENT FROM COVENTRY: LOCAL BANDS SET THE TONE!

CHAPTER 1

Coventry's 2 Tone bands had a flying start to the new decade with the Specials at number one in January 1980. The lyrics for Too Much too Young didn't pull any punches - it was about teenage pregnancy.

Rat Race later reached number five. Stereotypes/ International Jet Set was also a hit, as well as Do Nothing/ Maggie's Farm.

Selecter's Three Minute Hero, written by Neol Davies, reached number 16 in 1980 with local musician Joe Reynolds in the line-up.

"I played sax in a soul/reggae band called Stax in the early eighties, doing mainly funk/soul covers. I was also getting a fair amount of session work,

most notably the sax part on Three Minute Hero."

Despite their fame, some people still spelled the band's name wrong, including Warwick University's student newspaper! Perhaps we can forgive the budding journalists as they were giving away tickets for Selecter's January gig at Tiffany's.

Selecter

Sent From Coventry

The Specials and Selecter were major players but many other bands were bubbling away in what seemed the unlimited pool of Coventry's musical talent.

There was a lot of swapping of band members, making it hard to keep track of who was playing in which outfit. It really didn't matter, though, as collectively they offered a great variety of sounds whether at gigs or recording studios.

Trev Teasdel: "Bands proliferated in the wake of punk and 2 Tone. There was still much music industry interest in Coventry."

Local band Urge with Lynda Wulf on vocals and Rick Medlock

Dave Gedney, Urge

Dave Wankling, Urge

CONSUMER DISK   BOBBY

LOCAL BAND NIGHT
THE URGE
plus THE MIX

A band with a pedigree who have been slightly overlooked in the two-tone onslaught. They've been play-ing in their present line-up for eighteen months and the line-up includes Billy, from The Squad, drums, and two members of "Trans-Men" who used to boast Noel ... s of The Selecter and Brad from ... pecials amongst their number. ... ng term deal with Arista Records ... just been finalised, and their ... single on that label is due ... release in the new year. The ... le "Revolving Boy" on their own ... sumer" label sold heavily around ... area and nationwide in independ-... record shops but has now been ... idrawn for re-release, after re-mixing, in March.

You can see the guitar, bass, drums vocals and sax of The Urge in the DISCO ROOM on TUESDAY 25th NOVEMBER entry 50p. The support is, again, playing for love not money - The Mix

The vibrancy of it all spurred musician Martin Bowes into action, plenty of it. Martin was editor of the city's first fanzine, Alternative Sounds and also had his own band, Attrition.

"Coventry was going through the most exciting period of local music we have ever had. I knew a lot of bands through my work on the fanzine and record companies would send me records for review. Many people were coming to Coventry and writing about the music scene and I was often asked about bands and trends."

NEWS
RACIST MURDER

Last Friday over 1000 people attended the funeral of the young Asian murdered in a racist attack in Coventry. Satnam Singh Gill was stabbed in an attack by a group of skinheads as he walked through the main shopping precinct in the city centre at 2.00pm on Easter Saturday with his white girlfriend. A 16 year old youth has been charged with the murder, another with aiding and abetting and three more with making an affray.

3.00pm, when a gang of about 50, British Movement Organised skinheads attacked the demonstration chanting "Siegheil". Police moved in and about 30 arrests were made, 11 of them of anti-racists. Skinheads were again present at a further demonstration last Saturday but a large police presence and the fact that it was cup-final day prevented the tense atmosphere breaking into violence. Superintendent Ian McCardle of the Coventry police has appealed for calm, expressing his sympathy with the feelings of Coventry Asians "Over the unfortunate death", but stres-

Demonstration
A national demonstration, called by Coventry Committee against Racism and supported by the Indian Workers Association of Great Britain The National Union of Students and The Anti Nazi League, will take place in Coventry on Saturday May 23rd: Marchers will march from Foleshill, where Satnam Singh Gill a 20 year old student at Henley College, lived, to the city centre Meanwhile a further demonstration will take place next Saturday in the precinct.

Disgust

Martin saw other cities were coming up with their own albums and thought Coventry should definitely have one. "I knew the Cherry Red label through the fanzine so approached them with the idea of putting together a compilation album to celebrate local talent."

Cherry Red were interested and the result was the Sent From Coventry album, released in 1980. Many of the eleven bands featured on it had no recording experience when they turned up at the Woodbine Studios in Leamington Spa. But it all came together and the album sold thousands.

One of the bands featured was Urge, tipped for stardom after having toured in the late 1970s with the Specials. They played at many local venues including Warwick University. The student newspaper described them as "a band with a pedigree who have been slightly overlooked in the 2 Tone onslaught."

In 1980 they produced Revolving Boy on their own Consumer Disk label with band singer David Wankling writing the lyrics. John Peel was so impressed he showcased the single on his radio show, calling it "Coventry genius."

Val Haudiquet: "I went to see them as much as possible, mainly 'cos singer Dave was just beautiful! I am far from alone in that opinion."

They then signed with Arista and Bobby was released. The band split in 1981 then reformed with a few new, as well as former, band members - a practice that was quite common back then. Fame

proved elusive but they made an impression on the local scene as did scores of other home-grown bands.

Meanwhile, back in the big time, the Specials released the iconic Ghost Town, in 1981, their last before they split. Had it all been a bit 'too much, too young'? Before going their own ways, they organised a Peaceful Protest against Racism concert at the Butts stadium after the shocking racist murder of 20 year-old Satnam Singh.

Mike Lewis: "The Specials probably did more for black and white race relations than any government managed!"

The band wanted to unite people against racism and raise money for Satnam's family who lived in Foleshill. Nick Edgington was there.

"We drank in the Albany where the young Indian guy had been stabbed to death outside a few weeks before. Many thought the far right would gather there and it would kick off. We were warned to stay away. We had a few in the Fob Watch then made our way to the Albany, but nothing much happened.

"It turned out to be the Specials last Coventry gig before they split. I remember Coventry's Reluctant Stereotypes and Hazel O'Connor going down well. Then, as the sun was setting, the Specials started Ghost Town as their finale. The police stepped forward on the railway bridge behind the stage, silhouetted in the twilight. It sent shivers down our spines!"

Coventry music historian Pete Chambers was also there and had a similar spine-shivering moment. Pete was a huge Specials fan and on a

Coventry's own Hazel O'Connor wows the crowd at the Butts anti-racism concert 1981

mission to document 2 Tone in pictures and in words.

"The Butts gig felt like the end of something as the NF had marched in the city centre on the day. The People and Reluctant Stereotypes got us excited. Then as it grew dark Hazel O'Connor sat on the end of the stage, her legs dangling, and sang a spine tingling version of Will You, just as it began to drizzle."

Meryl Barrett wasn't actually at the concert but participated nevertheless. "I was sitting in my garden in Earlsdon not so far away listening to almost every word being sang!"

Pete Chambers: *"It was a moment in time, as the Specials took the stage, and told us why we were there, why black and white must unite. We hoped they would go on forever. I mean, how many bands split after a number one single? Sadly, it would come to pass. It was the very last time that the original Specials would play in their home city. Their swansong Ghost Town became a lot more real that night."*

Hazel O'Connor had already made a name for herself as an actress in the 1980 film Breaking Glass and also as a singer/ songwriter. She had hits with tracks she composed for Breaking Glass. Maxine Smyth loved Eighth Day, one of these tracks, and saw the film at the Coventry Odeon, as did many others.

Hazel was a local girl made very good indeed and still only at the start of a long, creative and successful career. Music clearly ran in the family as before her success, older brother Neil was doing well with a local band called the Flys.

John Docker: *"Loved Breaking Glass! Saw Hazel O'Connor perform it live at Coventry Theatre when I was about 16. I'd saved my paper round money and had a ticket downstairs at the theatre."*

The Flys cut a single, Molotov Cocktail, and appeared on John Peel's show and the Old Grey Whistle Test. Brother and sister sometimes worked alongside each other and even did covers of each other's songs! Neil did a version of Will You and Hazel had her own take on Molotov Cocktail.

The Reluctant Stereotypes were a local band Warwick University's Student Union actively promoted. They played support to the Q Tips at their Fresher's Ball in October 1980. The reviewer for student newspaper The Boar wrote:

"The band, looking like arts school boys in boiler suits and make-up, brought their own followers and had their own party. They brought the

Hazel O'Connor on stage at the Butts anti-racism gig 1981

Coventry sound back home, an eclectic fusion of jazz, rock, ska and reggae rhythms, sounding like Benny Goodman meeting the Specials in a concrete jungle. They earned their encore."

David Glibert went to college with Stereotypes member Paul Sampson and followed his earlier band, Bung.

"I made and have the only known recording of them live at the Walsgrave pub. Their song Cartomancy provided the first few moments of the Stereotypes Back to the Greek."

David Gilbert: *"The 'uniforms' worn by the Reluctant Stereotypes when they appeared on the Old Grey Whistle Test came from Coventry's Walsgrave Hospital!"*

The band released three singles in 1980: She Has Changed (Not You), Confused Action and Plans for Today.

Another local outfit that did well but didn't make it big were EMF- Electro Motive Force. Trev Teasdel thought they were "a great little band" with Tony 'Mojo' Morgan helping to bring the seven-piece band together. One of the tracks, a CND song called Ante-Bellum made it onto the Battle of the Bands album and became a single for RCA. Local photographer John Coles took the cover picture. EMF toured all over the country and supported bands like the Specials and the Beat.

Bands were constantly forming, splitting and reforming in different guises. Just like Doctor Who, the Specials 'regenerated' several times so the music just kept on coming. Special AKA performed and recorded between 1982 and 1984 with original and new members involved.

Rhoda Dakar was on vocals for The Boiler with Jerry Dammers on keyboard and John Bradbury drums. They were still courting controversy, the theme this time being date rape. Banned from Radio 1, it still made it to the charts.

On a lighter note, was Jungle Music with the line up that included internationally acclaimed Cuban ska and reggae trombonist Rico Rodriguez.

Terry Hall formed Fun Boy Three with Lynval Golding and Neville Staple from the Specials. They reached number 20 in 1981 with The Lunatics (have taken over the Asylum.)

Combining their efforts with Bananarama, they got to number four in February 1982 with It Ain't What You Do It's the Way that You Do It. They also recorded Really Saying Something with Bananarama, another hit in 1982.

When asked why they linked up with Bananarama, Terry Hall's tongue-in-cheek reply was that it was because they were just as talentless as them! Clearly the opposite was true, both groups being very talented, as their combined and individual hits show.

With The More I See the Less I Believe, Fun Boy

Three didn't fare so well, reaching just 68. Pete Chambers describes it as a "brave attack on the sad/mad situation in Northern Ireland."

Colourfield was Terry Hall's next band with Karl Shale and Toby Lyons, previously of the Swinging Cats, in the line-up. Colourfield's most successful single Thinking of You, reached number 12 in 1985.

Jerry Dammers kept himself busy and in 1984 released a single that was the accompaniment to many demonstrations for years to come: Free Nelson Mandela. This unofficial anti-apartheid anthem sent a clear message to the South African government and its supporters.

And so it was that 2 Tone faded but didn't disappear, with all the hits, and the fun, still coming.

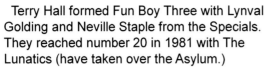

Local band Reluctant Stereotypes performing at Butts anti-racism concert in 1981

NIGHTCLUB NAUGHTINESS AT THE APOLLO, TIFFANY'S AND BUSTERS

T he entertainment just kept on coming at the Coventry Apollo Theatre - and it wasn't just happening on the stage!

A bit of saucy stuff went on in the audience at some gigs as Nick Edgington recalls.

"I was at the Cure gig with my girlfriend of the time, both of us dressed up as New Romantics. We sat near the front and the bass bins. When they played A Forest, the vibrations went right through us. My girlfriend claimed she had an orgasm!"

When Hot Chocolate appeared in 1982, there was further naughtiness amongst the audience. Mike Lewis remembers the first six rows of mostly female fans almost suffocating lead singer Errol Brown.

"They removed their knickers en masse and launched them at him at the same time. These days something like that would go viral on YouTube in hours!"

> **Joe Reynolds:** *"The early eighties were vibrant and a lot of live venues opened and closed in the city."*

Younger audiences were starting to find the thrill of the venue, Sid Wilson among them.

"My first and second gigs were the Stranglers at the Coventry Theatre, or whichever name it was then. Being only 11 and 13, my mum took me to both. I was standing on the back seats having a great time oblivious to anything else going on around me. Even a rumour going round that someone had a gun didn't faze me!"

Young punk Sid Wilson in early 80s

Aged just nine, Sid had taken the Stranglers Rattus Norvegicus album to the barbers on Tile Hill Lane. He pointed at JJB (Jean-Jacques Burnel) and told him: "Cut my hair like that!'"

> **Mike Lewis:** *"When Stranglers lead singer Hugh Cornwell had enough of being spat on, he shouted at the crowd, 'anyone else ** gobs on me and we are off.' Someone managed a ten-foot long disgusting projectile and off they went. There was virtually a riot!"*

Crowd trouble was not unheard of when the Stranglers played, with the odd arrest or two. The Stranglers 1981 gig was part of their Meninblack Tour.

> **Nick Edgington:** *"The Stranglers! One of my favourite bands. I went to see them on their Black and White album, which featured Nice n Sleazy. I was seated near the back and had a great view of David Greenfield (who I wanted to be) on his keyboards. 'Proper punks' weren't supposed to like them as they were 'too old' and could actually play their instruments but I loved their sound. My mother heard me one time playing their version of Walk On By and was in tears - it was my late father's favourite song."*

There was a minor outbreak of Osmondmania when the family group from Utah appeared in 1980. Pete Clemons' wife, a big fan, was caught up in that. She saw the band, bought a scarf and has kept it in pristine condition to this day.

> **John Docker:** *"Saw quite a few gigs at Coventry Theatre back in the day but Hazel O'Connor springs to mind. She did all the favourites from her Breaking Glass film soundtrack."*

Richard King's first ever gig was at the Apollo so he remembers it well. Kid Creole and the Coconuts gave the audience a taste of their tropical party time music, as part of their Tropical Gangsters album tour. Lee O'Hara saw the Style Council and General Public there but had to

Momento of the Osmonds concert in 1980

Tiffany's - top
night spot
captured by
Bill Boswell

DEREK BLOCK PRESENTS...

THE RUTS
PLUS SPECIAL GUESTS
THE VIBRATORS AND THE GAS
TIFFANY'S-THURS FEB 28
8.00PM

Tickets: 2.50 available from box office 0203
24570, Virgin Records, Poly and also on night

THE LAST SUPPER AT TIFFANYS

get his money back when Haircut 100 split up and cancelled.

Abbe Humphreys: "I went to lots of gigs there. Saw Gary Numan just when he released Cars. Genesis, Hawkwind, Buzzcocks, Gillan and many others."

Birmingham band UB40 played there in December 1984. Some remember getting in cheaper with proof of unemployment - a UB40. The band preferred working on a shoestring and avoided signing with a record company to keep their artistic freedom. Like the Specials, they had a multi-racial line up and were committed to anti-racism.

Joe Reynolds: "I saw Dr Feelgood at the Apollo, also ELO and Raymond Froggat."

It was not only bands appearing at the Apollo. The Two Ronnies did a Christmas show over December 1980/ January 1981 and Rowan Atkinson appeared as part of his 1981 Six City tour.

Comedian Jim Davidson didn't have much to laugh about during his time at the theatre in 1983, having dropped a paving slab on his foot on Christmas day. The show must go on, as they say, and like a trooper he hobbled back on stage, minus a shoe, in early January. Although in severe pain during the show on January 2nd, he bravely completed the performance. But he couldn't complete the show's run, which finished 11 days early.

Even with big names appearing, Coventry Theatre didn't survive the worsening economic conditions of the decade. Barbara Dickson gave the final concert in 1985, after which it became a bingo hall for a few years. Despite efforts to save it, the theatre was later demolished.

Local music writer Pete Clemons praises the great variety of concerts at the Apollo that catered for all tastes and ages. Pete saw its closure as a major loss for Coventry and wonders if the city ever recovered.

Not far from away was Coventry's other theatre, built in the postwar period - the Belgrade. Opened in 1958, it was named after Coventry's sister city in Yugoslavia (now Serbia) and housed more than a theatre. It ran the Depot studios where musicians could try out their music. Gigs also took place at the Belgrade and many local bands played there including Attrition, headed by Martin Bowes who was very active on the Coventry scene in the early '80s.

Local band Attrition headed up by Martin Bowes playing their first gig at the Belgrade Theatre, December 8th 1980

The soundtrack of the Human League was a constant throughout much of the decade

Top gigs at Tiff's

The Locarno had been one of Coventry's favourite venues since 1960 but by the 1980s was called Tiffany's, or just Tiff's for short.

Pete Clemons: "As punk rock/new wave, then ska took hold of the country in the late 1970s and into the early 1980s it became almost compulsory for bands to play Tiffany's. We saw the Clash, the Stranglers, XTC, Blondie, the Specials, Selecter, UB40 and the Undertones all hold court. The list was almost endless as Tiffany's became one of the nation's major venues."

Gala Bingo at the former Coventry Theatre late 1980s

For some bands, the experience was not so positive. Local DJ Toby Davies was on "humping/security duty" when Adam and the Ants played Tiff's, December 1980. The support was Coventry's God's Toys, who had a large local following, the Toy's Army.

"God's Toys had the plugs pulled on them as they had run over time - nothing to do with them going down great!"

Nick Edgington: *"Adam and the Ants' roadies pulled the plug on God's Toys before they'd finished. Not a happy band or crowd!"*

Toby and his two colleagues had to draw up a guard rota for the Ants van as it had been bricked the night before in Cardiff.

"Adam and the Ants were so disappointing that three of us ended up in there. We helped ourselves to the band's post-gig refreshments which were hidden under the seats!"

After the gig, two young girls begged to be concealed in a flight case as a way of meeting Adam. "I had to point out that they'd be discovered by a roadie rather than Mr. Ant."

A student reviewer also noted the plug-pulling incident and was less than impressed by Adam.

"His shirt did predictably did come off though he managed to keep it on till the encore. Kings of the Wild Frontier was left for this, again quite predictably. This was played very badly as was You're So Physical. He made a patronising comment to the audience 'Coventry you're a sexy town' and that was it."

Nick Edgington saw UB40 at Tiff's for the first time.

"I loved their early stuff. I think the 1982 tour was one they opened with Red Red Wine. Great then but I am so tired of hearing it all round the world still, from Birmingham to Barbados!"

£2 would have bought a ticket to see the Pretenders in January 1980. The Clash came the following month. There was a spitting incident, and Joe Strummer launched himself into the crowd. One reviewer wrote: "Strummer fought Coventry's Joe Public and Strummer, on balance, won."

Other punk bands came, including the Ruts and the Vibrators.

When Selecter played to a scarcely quarter full

Tiffany's, some viewed it as a sign of 2 Tone's decline. But the ticket price, £3, had something to do with it. At a time when many were working short-time or on the dole, this was dear.

Reviewer Steve Rappaport noted Pauline Black's enthusiasm as she warmed up the audience. She was "evidently pleased to be playing live in front of a British audience again and of course, Coventry is special!"

May 1981 brought "the last supper at Tiffany's." The last to play there were Echo and the Bunnymen, with local Birmingham band the Photos supporting. They were quite good in the view of music writer Pete Clemons.

Another major venue disappeared for good, no more climbing those stairs to dance floor heaven. It reopened in 1986 as something completely different - the city's Central Library.

'Buster's Alternative' nights

Busters had various offerings for Dirty Stop Outs. Nick Edgington picked up free tickets from local

pubs the Bear or Rose and Crown for 'alternative' night. He figured the quickest route there was via a nearby car park.

"You would see punks, goths and all manner of weird folk scurrying through the car park. It was like a scene from a postmodern movie!"

Alan West was one of those "car park scurriers" on his way to Busters. Rob Summerfield was a "bit of an indie type for while" so he also headed to the "cave-like" Busters on Tuesday nights.

Arnold William remembers that cave-like decor, probably a throwback to its days as the Forty Thieves.

"Since it was first built, no matter what its name or admissions policy, the management kept the glass fibre imitation caves."

Richard King, a young lady and Busters cave-like interior

Nick Edgington and friend in cave-like Busters nightclub

Kate Hart and a friend in the very cave-like Busters

Sid Wilson: *"Busters always stumped me as, when it was free to get in, and cheap drinks, it was only half-full. When it cost to get in, and the beer was full price, it was rammed!"*
Nick Edgington met his wife-to-be in Busters, which he thought was more alternative than elsewhere in town even at weekends.
"No crappy disco allowed! My wife was actually more into rock but still preferred Busters to the 'townie' joints. There was no real dress code on alternative night."

This was very much appreciated by Arnold William. "I was allowed in even with my normal scruffiness, unlike the City Centre nightclub where I once was asked to leave for wearing wellies!"

Park Lane was another popular nightspot. Formerly known as Mr George's, it had pioneered local 2 Tone and punk bands in the late 1970s. In the eighties, it tried to be a bit more sophisticated (their might be a hint in that name!) and served meals.

Other nightspots included La Chaumiere in the Burges, with live music as well as discos. It was one of the venues Joe Reynolds played at in local band Stax, a soul/reggae outfit. They also did slots at the Commonwealth Club in Lockhurst Lane.

Smaller venues did a great job in providing amazing nights of all sorts. But the closure of the 'giants' such as Coventry Theatre and Tiffany's hit the city's Dirty Stop Outs hard.

MEETING YOUR OTHER HALF, MAKING MUSIC & THE FAR GOSFORD STREET RUN:COVENTRY'S PUBS

Coventry's pubs were great for meeting friends, checking out fashions and even finding the love of your life! And did someone mention beer?

Mark Rewhorn met his ex-wife in the popular Port O Call in Earlsdon. Her first words to him were, "Will you lot shut up, I'm trying to talk to my mate! Oh, you look nice!" One thing led to another and they got married.

Nick Edgington spent many happy nights at the Alhambra, Silver Sword and Black Eagle with one lot of mates, and the Bear, Rose and Crown, or the Albany in Earlsdon with others. He clearly had a lot of mates!

David Gilbert: "The Port O Call had great Sunday night discos in 1981/2. I worked there and it was rammed. Four deep at the bar!"

Rob Summerfield's local haunt was the Bulls Head on the Binley Road. "There were some great, ram-packed disco nights there!" He also frequented city centre pubs: the Silver Sword, Alhambra, Penny Black and Three Tuns.

Pubs were also cracking music venues as local music promoters, such as Ken Brown at the General Wolfe, offered a stage for bands to try out their tunes.

One street had so many pubs that 'crawl' was far from the right word - it became known as a run! Far Gosford Street had many fans including Steve Ashwell who went to live in the area.

"There were 13 pubs between the Colin Campbell and what we used to call the 'ancient testicle', the Old Ball. There was the Oak, Colin Campbell, Hand and Heart - pubs all the way up! We liked to just have a pint then move on. You'd go to one pub and know everybody. Then the next pub, same thing."

Arnold William became another 'Fargo run' fan after flat mate Paddy, who worked at the Lanchester Poly, introduced him to it.

"We would stop at each pub for a half pint, get that chucked down our necks before starting to

Anne Porter (in black) and friends take their fab hair on a night out at the Colin Campbell pub, 1985

The grand old man of pubs- Sir Colin Campbell, famed for its gigs

Engrossed in their air guitars at the Colin Campbell!

drink proper. The run started at the Pitts Head then the Hand and Heart, missing out the Golden Cup for some reason then the Peacock, the Oak and the Campbell."

After that, things tended to get a bit "confused," which is perhaps not surprising!

"The Oak Inn was popular with art students and certain 'old hippy' types. The back room was often scented with aromatic tobacco. Many a student party started after closing time at the Oak with brisk off-sales of Breaker as well as cider bottles filled with bitter from the tap."

Perhaps one of them might have been at Gillian Dawson's place as she was a big fan of the Oak.

"Student days were spent in the Oak. It was then usually back to mine to carry on the party as I lived nearest the pub."

Rich Mulligan's version of the Gosford Street run had the Hertford Arms at the 'top.' Another big starting place was the White Lion, just round the corner.

Nick Edgington met friends at the Colin Campbell, played pool and went to the upstairs gigs.

The Pilgrims played there, another great Coventry band in Nick's view, with Greg Crabb their charismatic lead singer.

"When they played sober they were really good. But if they decided to have a few drinks, they changed their name to the Raggle Taggle Gypsies. They were much funnier."

Roy Lenton enjoyed DJing there in the late eighties along with Pete Lawrence and Paul Gough.

Rockabilly fan Alan West thought the Coventry scene was "awesome".

"There were so many gigs and venues, including the Old Ball, Hand and Heart, the Campbell, and Brew and Baker. Between 1980 and 1982 I was

Adrian Chadwick: *"The Oak was run by an Irish couple Jim and Babs and there was also a barmaid called Margaret. It wasn't a 'lock-in' as such but you always got about 45 minutes drinking up time. Went on to many parties afterwards in Stoke and Hillfields.*

The often visited and much loved Alhambra pub

One of the many popular pubs on Far Gosford Street

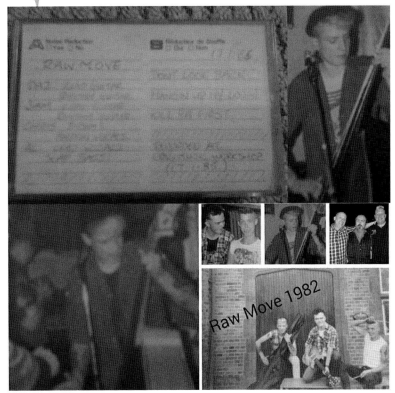

Raw Move 1982

Musician Alan West who played in Raw Move in 1980s and rockabilly fan and musician Alan West and his famous quiff (and guitar) today

going to rockabilly gigs and discos five nights a week. This didn't go down too well with my parents!"

Closer to the city centre, juost off High Street, was the popular Rose and Crown, one of Coventry's oldest pubs dating back to the early 1600s.

> **Rose Hart:** *"The Rose and Crown was my local. Loved it. I used to play in the pool team. Loved walking, clip clopping more like, up the cobbles from Pool Meadow in my pixie boots. Summers spent there, just watching people with friends, seeing who's around, being seen! Then hurrying down to the Dog and Trumpet."*

Sid Wilson would queue to get in on Sunday mornings after particularly drunken Saturday evenings. Rich Mulligan recalls a "hair of the dog" or two there, straight from a party.

"This was very common when pubs closed early and you didn't want to wear the white shirt, tie, shoes uniform of the nightclubs."

Coventry's punks, including Rich, liked the Rose and Crown.

"The punk/ alternative/goth crowds gradually displaced the gay crowd in the Rose and Crown in the days before a pub could officially be a gay bar. Most 'alternative' pubs and club nights began in gay venues, as they were the most open minded and welcoming. The majority of pubs simply did not let you in with leathers or coloured hair. And if they did, you took your chances with the city centre crowds."

A sneaky visit to the Rose and Crown one day

cost local musician Alan West his five minutes of fame.

"My first band Raw Move played at an all-day event in 1983 with many bands from Coventry bands and Bologna, a town twinned with the city. The event brought together young people interested in music. Myself and two other band members decided to have a cheeky few beers at the Rose and Crown. During our getaway the local press arrived. As our guitarist didn't drink, he had stayed behind so enjoyed the photo opportunity with my upright bass!"

Kate Hart with friends in her favourite pub - the Rose and Crown

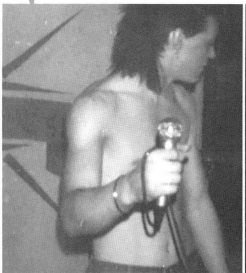

Steve Guest getting warmed up at the Rose and Crown and with the band performing there

What's in a name?

Sue Lowe somehow fitted in work between lunchtimes and evenings spent at the Hare and Squirrel in Cow Lane.

"Local singer Don Fardon (of Indian Reservation fame) ran the pub before moving to the Alhambra."

Arnold William remembers the Climax in the Arcade being the only pub with a racing car engine on display - the Climax engine. Col Hughes played guitar in a band called Siren in the early 1980s and they did gigs upstairs.

> **Lyn Farnell:** *"I just want to be taken back to the Climax on a Friday and Saturday night!"*

The Climax reopened as the Bug and Black Bat in January 1984.

Nick Edgington was none too keen on the Climax because of trouble between punks and teds.

"It all calmed down as the Big and Black Bat became very popular. So popular, in fact, that I had my wedding do there in 1986. I struggled to choose the 'our tune' to start the dancing. The DJ suggested Chris Dr Burgh's Woman in Red, so I

told him he was sacked! We should have gone for Let's Stick Together by Roxy Music but ended up with Spandau Ballet."

Arnold William remembers the landlord, Colum Nugent, who was "much loved by Coventry rock and roll revivalists and kept a well-run pub."

The Summerland Tavern in the Butts also got a new name. It underwent a £75,000 facelift in 1981 and the Coventry Evening Telegraph ran a competition to find a new name. Over 1600 readers sent in their ideas and the one selected was Mrs. Heather Spencer's.

Heather had heard the pub would be serving Flowers Old Bitter and took the FOB from that then thought of the former watch making industry in the area. The Fob Watch was Heather's winning result and she was invited to the pub's VIP reopening.

Even as a baby Sue Lowe could sniff out a pub! This one is the Burnt Post

Sue Lowe and her friend on a night out at the Jules Verne theme pub with an exotic drink!

The 'Dive Boys'

The Lady Godiva pub in Jordan Well, the 'Dive,' was the destination for local rockers, Col Hughes among them. Many of them played one instrument or another and formed bands, Col included.

"We rockers didn't conform to the norm. Rock music wasn't just our taste in music, it was our way of life! We lived it all the time with the long hair, jeans, T-shirt probably with a band name on and denim jacket with badges and sewn on patches or maybe a velvet jacket and desert boots. I was never interested in nightclubs. It was the Dive for us. We never took any notice of punk or 2 Tone. The Dive was definitely a rock pub."

Just outside the city centre was the Freemason's Arms. Musician Ray Jenkins, whose dad Martin was also a well-known musician, remembers it fondly.

"The Freemasons was run by Marg and Gordon Morgan, 'salt of the earth' type of people, very well respected. Their passion for live music and people made the pub very special. Tony, their son, was also a musician and took me under his musical wings."

Ray Jenkins: "We had great times at the Freemasons Arms. It was one of the best music venues. Lots of great musicians played there and it was always chocker-block with people from all walks of life and musical tastes having a great night."

Gillian Dawson never missed a music session when in the area, especially when Quiet Riot was on. This was a collective of musicians mainly consisting of Dando Shaft members including John Martyn, Bert Jansch and Tony Capstick.

When Mark Rewhorn lived nearby he spent many great nights there. "I floated home after a couple of pints. Goodness knows what they put in the beer!"

The Foresters was another popular Hillfields pub with music and parties. Pub lover Gillian Dawson used to go to 'Paddy's Folk Night' there then back to his to carry on drinking.

Col Hughes with Siren at the Climax

1981

Col Hughes in full guitar mode upstairs at the Climax

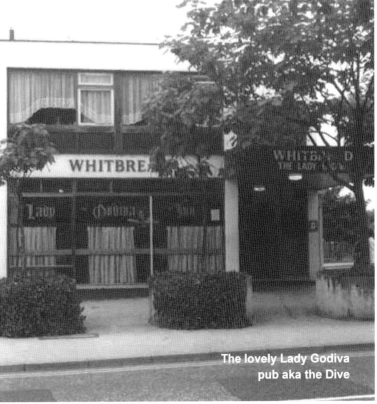

The lovely Lady Godiva pub aka the Dive

Arnold William recalls the Wednesday night sessions in the back room "for those who enjoyed performing and 'community singing' not to mention drinking!"

Suburban pubs thrived and many had brisk weekday lunchtime trade if they were near one of the city's many workplaces such as British Leyland in Canley or Jaguar in Allesley.

Pubs and alcohol, especially at lunchtimes, featured majorly for those at work in the 1980s according to Sue Lowe. She joined Massey Ferguson workmates for 'Monday Moans' at a local pub to ease into the week and they always went out for a lunchtime drink on Fridays.

"We went to the Standard, the Unicorn, the Bell, the Peeping Tom, Brickmakers' Arms, the Newlands, the Woodlands, plus lots more, all within easy reach of Massey Ferguson."

The Red Lion over at Walsgrave was one of Colin Horton's favourite pubs.

"In the 1980s it was rammed every Sunday and Monday nights, you couldn't get parked anywhere nearby. Our eyes were running from the smoke but great times!"

Sue Lowe was over that way on Thursday evenings after work.

"We used to go ten pin bowling at Forum Bowl on Walsgrave Road then have a couple of drinks at the Walsgrave pub afterwards. Great evenings, fuelled by double gin and tonics, ordered and consumed by the most highly paid person there. Dylan, a golden Labrador, was usually there, eating a packet of crisps. My 26th birthday present was a pointer so we named him Dylan!"

Over in Grayswood Avenue, there was a Jules Verne themed pub. Sue Long remembers going there and thinking it was very exciting!

"There were different themed bars – one Western themed with swing doors, one with an actual prow of a ship with barrels to sit on, a hot air balloon suspended from the ceiling... you get the gist! They did exotic drinks as well to go with the themes."

In 1988 Coventry Council became the first to pass a by-law prohibiting the consumption of alcohol anywhere in public in the city centre. It was later rolled out across the whole of Coventry.

Chris Wilson wrote in the 'Street Talk' column of the Evening Telegraph that this ban was "such a waste of time," and "taking a sledgehammer to crack a nut. The drunken activities of young yobs can be easily curtailed using the wide-reaching powers of the Public Order Act."

Pressures were put on pubs as well with the council bringing in a Pub Watch and identity card scheme to deal with problems related to underage drinking. It was common for young people to socialise in pubs but the council wanted to change this culture.

For some, this was also taking things too far and started to take some of the fun out of going around the many pubs of Coventry with their different subcultures, styles and music.

Welcoming in the New Year -1981- at the Dive!

20 year Col Hughes outside his favourite place- the Dive!

Col Hughes and friend outside the Dive

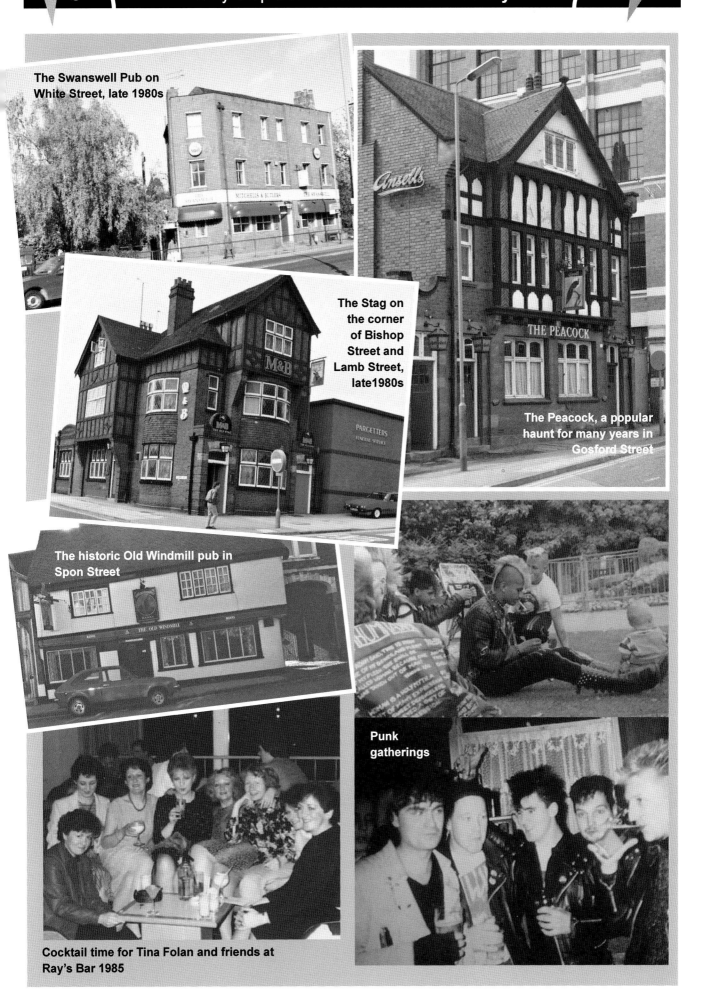

The Swanswell Pub on White Street, late 1980s

The Stag on the corner of Bishop Street and Lamb Street, late 1980s

The Peacock, a popular haunt for many years in Gosford Street

The historic Old Windmill pub in Spon Street

Punk gatherings

Cocktail time for Tina Folan and friends at Ray's Bar 1985

Left:
Col Hughes
enjoying a
night out
downstairs
at the
Lanch

BODY MUSIC・BODY MUSIC・BODY MUSIC

FUNK・JAZZ・LATIN・PERCUSSION・

EVERY FRIDAY FROM OCTOBER 1st 75p - 50p DOLE

COVENTRY POLY DOWNSTAIRS BAR

DANCING TILL MIDNIGHT

FILMIC INTERLUDE

refer to handbill

ARTS CENTRE BOX OFFICE COVENTRY (0203) 417417

HAL' EVE

DAY	DATE	MONTH	TIME
SAT	28TH	NOV	9.30

BILLIE JOE SPEARS: 2
* * * * * * * * * * * * * * * * *

DOOR	ROW	SEAT	PRICE
G	AA	15	3.00

PLE

Dill of God'sToys

The BIGGEST selection of entertainment in the Midlands this Autumn....

Saturday 30th September
BILLY ECKSTINE and FREDA
PAYNE

Tuesday 3 – Saturday 7 October
Tic Toc Theatre Company
SCHOOL'S OUT by Jon Gaunt

Monday 9 – Saturday 11
October
Temba Theatre Company
BACK STREET MAMMY by
Trish Cooke

Thursday 12 – Saturday 14
October
SHAKERS by John Godber

Friday 13 October
PETER SKELLERN AND THE
LITTLE BIG BAND

Monday 16th October
DANNY THOMPSON'S
WHATEVER
and TOUMANI DIABATE

Tuesday 24 – Saturday 28th
October
LONDON CONTEMPORARY
DANCE THEATRE

Monday 30th October
STEPHANE GRAPPELLI

Monday 13th – Saturday 18th
November
MACBETH

Monday 13th November
FRANKIE HOWERD

Wednesday 15th – Saturday
18th November
THE NORMAL HEART

Thursday 23rd November
RIK MAYALL

For full details of the Arts
Centre's programme and film
season, ring the ARTS
CENTRE BOX OFFICE
Coventry (0203) 417417

ARTS CENTRE

UNIVERSITY OF WARWICK

• Rik Mayall

EASTER BALL
DEXY'S MIDNIGHT RUNNERS
BAD MANNERS

THURS 13TH MARCH
UNION BUILDING
£1.00 ADV
£1.20 DOOR.

EASTER BALL – DEXY'S MIDNIGHT RUNNERS AND BAD MANNERS.

The Pascal festivities celebrating the end of the term
will no doubt be a night to remember. Headlining is
Dexy's Midnight Runners, described by Melody Maker as
"probably one of the loudest, strongest and most
convincing bands currently treading the boards". Their
brand of music is sweaty soul music, derived from Tamla
Mowtown and Stax sources "imbued with passion and energy
and delivered with an almost unnerving verve and pre-
cision. Their songs don't just beg to be danced to,'
they grab you and make you dance."

Support is new band Bad Manners, fronted by Fatty AKA
Buster Bloodvessel, the man with a thirteen inch tongue
backed by Gus Herman, trumpet, Marcus Absent, Saxophone,
Louis E. Robinson III, Rhytho guitar, Brian Chew-it,
Drums, Edward Bazoowiex, Tenor sax, Reggie Mental, bass,

Marston's
PROMOTION EVENING
THURSDAY 12 MARCH
Union Building 8.15 p.m.

PRIZES   GAMES

Pedigree

Pedigree

the bitter beer
with the true
English character

Pedigree

BREWED AT BURTON ON TRENT BY

Scottish & Newcastle

EVENING 15p

WEDNESDAY 3 DECEMBER

SOUL
in the
Union
DEXY'S MIDNIGHT
RUNNERS
THURSDAY

Pernod – sunfine evening
TUES 13 MAY
8-30 - 10-80
UNION
PERNOD –
– 25
Sunfine

PERNOD
the French way

disco

GOING TO UNI AND HAVING FUN IN THE 'BURBS

Many of those who regularly made their way over to Warwick University weren't going to lectures but great gigs and nights out!

The university had grown considerably by the 1980s with a very active Student's Union. The Butterworth Hall in the Arts Centre, completed in early 1981, could seat 1500.

Public transport had improved too, with buses going right into the university. Trev Teasdel recalls how you had to get off the bus on the Kenilworth Road and walk some way to campus before the change. This was a bit off-putting especially late at night.

"The Student Union ran minibuses back to Coventry on the nights when there were events on. They were mainly for students who lived in town but we used to get them anyway!"

Joe Reynolds: "I remember seeing Pamela Stevenson and Joseph and the Amazing Technicolour Dream Coat at the Arts Centre, Rico Rodrigues' band and Geno Washington at the Student's Union. Geno was enjoying a 'second coming' after the success of Geno by Dexy's Midnight Runners. Rico and Dick Cuthall were enjoying success due to the Specials. A lot of local bands played there as well such as the VIPs. Student Rag Weeks were still popular and a lot of acts played at the Rag Balls."

Ian Green remembers The Smiths appearing in Coventry twice in the same week in 1984.

"Once it was at the Lanch and then at Warwick Uni- incredible! I reckon they mixed the Lanch up with Lancaster and thought Warwick was in Warwick! Both great gigs anyhow."

The Lanch had been renamed Coventry Polytechnic in 1980 but locals carried on using its old name.

Pete Clemons: "If the 1970s saw some major talent play Warwick University then it has to be said that the 1980s saw a real purple patch for the university as both the ever growing Arts Centre and the Student's Union were attracting some serious names and a host of local bands such as King and the Specials."

The list of bands who played there is, in Pete's words, "quite substantial, absolutely staggering." Think of any band from that era and the likelihood is they played Warwick at some point! From the Stranglers to Simply Red, U2 to UB40, REM to the Reluctant Stereotypes, the Specials to Bow Wow Wow.

Gary Masterson went to see U2 there.

"A great gig! It was before October came out and after Boy. Seen some other great bands at the Uni. I grew up in nearby Canley so it was our weekend haunt."

Stuart Beamish used to pop over and enjoyed the Tom Robinson Band.

"Really good set, quite political and Power in the Darkness a fantastic track. I didn't know them previously and went on a friend's advice. They came back out to do an encore and that is probably the only time I have been in a room with 200+ people all pogo-ing and shouting 'Sing if you're glad to be gay!'"

Gigs and other events at Warwick's SU were often facilitated by 'specials' on certain drinks with promotions from the breweries. It could be a beer, lager or even Pernod, all offered at lower prices to encourage punters to try them out.

The Student's Union was good at promoting local bands, not just the big names. God's Toys, with lead singer Dill (Stephen Davies) played there several times and their set at the New Year's Ball

God's Toys in action and two of their singles

GODS TOYS

in January 1980 went down well. William Leith reviewed the gig:

"Camp and arty, histrionic and bizarre, an act that's courageously followed its own nose through the Midlands maze, arriving at a point somewhere between enthusiasm and competence, a large following and no contract, professional and sheer manic romp. Exit and encore to tumultuous applause!"

Pete Chambers described the band as Coventry's "own little secret."

Warwick welcomed back the band in March and received odd praise. "God's Toys are Coventry's answer to a wet March night- dependable as Horlicks, quirk, strangeness and charm."

Val Haudiquet confirms all that.

"Dill! We went to the local launderette one day off Albany Road, with a Dylon fabric dye 'cos he wanted all his clothes to be purple. God help the poor person who used that machine after us."

Nick Edgington remembers Dill from school and once hired God's Toys for a birthday bash. "At the party, the big dance floor fillers were Tom Robinson Band's 2-4-6-8 Motorway and Sing if you're glad to be gay! Great stuff!"

David Gilbert liked and bought both God's Toys singles, All the Born Losers (1980) and Everybody's got a Mother (1981).

Another reviewer wrote how well God's Toys had done considering that they'd been voted Coventry's fifth worst band in an Alternative News poll! "Who'd have thought they'd become famous?" he asked. But they split up before they really made it big.

The university even had its own bands with some doing quite nicely! The VIPs were one of these and local musician Joe Reynolds played on some of their records. The VIPs formed at Warwick in 1978 and won the student union's talent contest.

The band turned professional and headed to London where they performed at just about every major venue over the next two years. They were unlucky in having their Top of the Pops appearance cancelled due to a technician's strike. When lead singer Jed Dmochowski decided he'd had enough of the strain of touring with the band, they did their farewell gig at Coventry's General Wolfe pub.

If the student crowd wasn't your cup of tea, very close to Warwick University was a small club called Corners. Kevin Gill thought Corners was a "great little club," situated in the clubhouse of Coventry Sporting FC. "

Stuart Beamish: *"Went to several parties at Corners when I had friends at nearby Canley Teacher's training college. I recall one St. Trinians party when I went as a schoolgirl. Yep, it was scary!"*

Joe Reynolds saw Warwick's emergence as a live venue as one to rival the Lanch Poly, which had been the main place to go in the previous two decades. The Lanch still offered good bands and DJs, plus their followers and had some interesting characters.

DJ Toby Davies remembers a Gary Numan look-alike who was a regular at the Lanch downstairs bar on Saturdays in early 1980s.

"When DJs Lof and Tim Strickland played a Numan tune, the whole floor would clear as this guy performed his trance-like dance and there was often applause at the end. Bizarre! Think he was called Adrian. Those Saturday's were a healthy mix of students and locals."

The Thompson Twins played the Lanch in February 1981 to an almost empty hall. A review praised them for their efforts given the low turnout. "The Thompson Twins succeeded in transforming the few wretched souls strewn around this large hall into a gyrating mass of bodies."

Wed

Strangers - Hope & Anchor, Whitefriars Lane, Cov. Singaround with Dave Bennett - Old Dyers Arms Spon End, Cov.

Thurs

Babylon Rebels - General Wolfe Foleshill Road, Coventry.

Fri

Rock Goddess & The Androids of Mu - General Wolfe

ROCK GODDESS, playing a date at the General Wolfe, Coventry, next week.

And over to the Wolfe!

Foleshill was an older part of Coventry, with redbrick terraced houses built for workers in the 19th century. There were also some old pubs for them as well and 1980s' Dirty Stop Outs loved one of them in particular: the General Wolfe on Foleshill Road.

It had become home to up-and-coming bands as well as better known ones. The Wolfe, as it was usually called, was a cracking music venue and landlord Ken Brown did much to promote the pub and the performers. He booked in many great bands, not only to the Wolfe but the Dog and Trumpet, making live music lovers very happy indeed.

Alan Joseph: "U2 played the Wolfe twice in the early eighties. The first time owner Ken Brown paid them £200. Second time around £400. The third time they wanted £750! Ken thought it was a lot so they ended up at the Lanch instead."

Julie with local band Attrition live at the General Wolfe 1984

Martin Bowes in action with Attrition at the General Wolfe 1984

THE GENERAL WOLFE
LIVE

Deja Vu + Support _____ Sat. 5

Major 5 +
    Wild and Wandering ____ Sat. 12

DT's +
    La Grange _____ Fri. 18

Cov Aid Lanchester Poly No live music at the Wolfe __ Sat. 19

Doc Mustard & The Cobalt Kid ____ Fri. 25
    + Support

Hawaiian Surgeons + Support _____ Sat. 26

October

THE GENERAL WOLFE
Foleshill Road, Coventry

The V.I.P'S farewell gig

VIPs farewell gig at General Wolfe

Toby Davies was at the U2 gig in September 6th 1980.

"It was by no means packed. About halfway through the set, I returned from the bar to my space fairly near the back of the room and became aware of some animated figure next to me. Bono! With the aid of an extra long microphone cable, he was now singing from the audience whilst facing the stage." Toby, however, wasn't impressed.

Another Wolfe regular was Gary Morton and he saw U2, as well as Robert Plant and Otway and Barrett. He was in the audience when the Eurythmics played there before they were famous.

The only band Nick Edgington saw there that went on to bigger things was Talk Talk. It was around 1984 he thinks, around the time they released their hit It's My Life.

Musician Alan West was playing in Rockabilly band Raw Move in 1982.

"We supported Johnny Wilde and the West at the General Wolfe, and later went on to form

The DTs at the Wolfe

The DTs at the Wolfe

Local band the Jolly Dwarves

The Trash Can Rebels with Coventry's well-known slap bass player Sam Smith and Baz Thompson."

Rob Summerfield was bass player in the Jolly Dwarfs who also graced the Wolfe's stage. Their local, however, was the Bulls Head on the Binley Road and they did their first gig there in the late eighties.

Their performances were usually very 'merry,' accompanied by lots of drinking. They were quite open in their criticism of the outdoor drinking ban brought in by the local council and this led to them being labelled as 'irresponsible." The beer and the gigs started to dry up and the band split.

The General Wolfe was a big draw in the eighties. It was part of the very varied mix of venues on offer, which included Warwick University and other suburban music pubs. Plenty on offer for Dirty Stop Outs willing to venture beyond the city centre!

Right: Jolly Dwarfs Desperation Tour T-shirt!

Rob and Ray of Jolly Dwarfs in action at the Bulls Head

The audience enjoying Jolly Dwarfs gig at the Bulls Head

The Round Café, shoppers and Tiffany's all nicely
captured by Bill Boswell

ROMANCE AT THE RAJAH AND OTHER CULINARY TALES

CHAPTER 5

Falling in love with curry was very easy to do in 1980s Coventry. Sharing a vindaloo was even known to lead to love, marriage and the next generation of curry lovers!

Whilst many still headed to the Parsons Nose for their famous 'one all in' takeaway, more adventurous Dirty Stop Outs liked to try foods from further beyond the city boundaries. Some were surprised by how easily they acquired a life-long curry habit.

It all began at the Rajah for Nick Edgington,

"One of my happy 1980s memories is the discovery of the joys of curry at the Rajah in the Burges. My first ever curry was in there, when a girl I was trying to chat up in the Alhambra pub invited me to join her and her friends. I struggled with a fear of curry versus young lust, but risked it, had my first visit to the Rajah, and fell in love. Not with the girl but with Indian food."

Later on Nick met a young lady who shared his spicy passion.

"As luck would have it, my next girlfriend, and wife to be, was a curry lover. We got into a routine at the weekends of going for a drink at the Albany then driving into town. We'd park behind the Tally Ho pub then go through the alley way into the Burges. Then we'd climb the stairs to curry heaven!"

Colin Horton also discovered he loved curry at the Rajah and, again, a young lady was involved.

"I went to Rajah for the first time in 1980 because of a girl. I had never eaten 'foreign muck' as my mum would say - we were strictly roast dinners. In fact a previous girlfriend said she loved coming to our house because we had Sunday dinner every day! I ordered chicken salad while this girl I later married tucked into a curry. It looked and smelt yummy so I tried a bit. I was hooked! We used to go there most Sundays for a ruby and late drinks. Great nights."

Nick Edgington: "The Rajah was really popular, mainly with locals wanting a late drink and putting up with the curry, so there was always a good atmosphere with happy drunks galore. A few used to try to do a runner without paying, so there were a couple of bouncers, but we rarely saw anything kicking off."

What is it about curry? Must be something in those spices that get people all warmed up.

As Nick and his wife were Rajah regulars, they were usually ushered into an alcove at the back of the restaurant, which the waiters called "the nice corner for nice people."

"We often shared this with Coventry City players and their WAGS. The food there was really good. I still rate their onion bhajis and special mint sauce the best ever, and the chicken rezala one of my all time favourites."

They were saddened to see it decline over the years and a change of name to Saffron didn't help much. They still miss it, as nothing has taken its place in their view and John D'Arcy agrees.

What is it about curry? Must be all those spices get people warmed up.

"I don't think I've ate a curry as nice as the Rajah's since, and there's been a few!"

Another popular Indian place was Raj Doot in the Arcade.

Whilst the Rajah was Lesley Hannah Murray's first curry house, she and her family became Raj Doot regulars.

"Married and with a little one, we'd get there at opening time as the manager used to open up and bring his little one in with him and both kids had a run around the tables. My daughter would have been about four and thankfully has grown up with a love of Indian food."

Nick Edgington's experience of the Raj Doot left him with more than a bad taste in his mouth.

"I had a meal involving chicken tikka in kheema mince that made me stink of curry the morning after. Unfortunately, my boss at the time at the GEC was a curry hater, and I'm sure the lingering aroma was one of the reasons he selected me for redundancy shortly after. The Raj Doot may have cost me my job!"

Local musician Joe Reynolds played in Stax who had a residency at the Jubilee Pub on the Stoney Stanton Road.

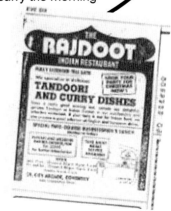

"This pub was run by Pele Bains who later ran the William IV on the Foleshill Road which was the first 'curry pub' in Coventry. Pele became famous for his curries and used to do 'guest appearances' at some of the local clubs for their curry nights."

Mr Bains was only 21 when he started his pub landlord career at the Phantom Coach in Canley. He's well known for turning the William IV into the first curry pub and doing similar transformations elsewhere. And his nickname Pele? Clearly because of his footballing prowess!

For some, it was Chinese food that got their taste buds tingling. Apart from popular Indian and Chinese restaurants, Coventry had its favourites from the previous decade: Roma Nello in the Arcade and the Swiss Alps.

There was a very sad ending for Nello's, open since 1973, when its owner drowned whilst on a family holiday in Rio de Janeiro. Nello Minelli had a heart attack whilst swimming, as his wife and children sat on the beach. His customers were saddened by Nello's tragic death.

There were other Italian eateries in the city and for those wanting to go a bit more upmarket, Da Vinci's in Earlsdon was the place to go. Sue Lowe and her husband went there, stopping at the Royal Oak on the way for a couple of drinks.

"It was the late eighties when we enjoyed Da Vinci's, a rather upmarket (and expensive) restaurant in Earlsdon's High Street. It was silver service with formally-dressed waiters who reminded me of Manuel from Fawlty Towers, and starched, snowy-white table cloths. The food was wonderful. I liked crab linguini in a light, creamy, white wine sauce, or, amazing tuna dressed with garlicky tomatoes and olives."

The Italian flavour could also be found at Etna Restaurant, which opened in 1981 in Hertford Street. They advertised themselves as 'a taste

Once a great taste of Sicily!

of Sicily.' With a name like Etna, they just had to have 'Volcano steaks' on the menu! Sue Lowe tried one and can't quite forget it being "wickedly hot with garlic and chilli." Wonder if they did lava soup for starters?

Somewhere more greasy spoon and open all hours was Noel's Café in Foleshill. For Rich Mulligan, it was a "Coventry institution" and the haunt of many music fans after late night gigs at the General Wolfe. "No-one dare nod off as you'd be straight out on the street!"

Tim Healey was there on New Years Eve 1980, after his band headlined at the General Wolfe. He remembers watching the Old Grey Whistle Test special on a small black and white telly in the all-night café.

Val Haudiquet was another of the café's customers.

"Being pretty much opposite the General Wolfe, it was handy."

Noel's was used as the venue for the video of a Special AKA single in 1982, Jungle Music, featuring Cuban-born trombonist Rico Rodriguez. Noel's café can be seen full of brightly dressed people dancing around to the catchy tune.

Back in the city, a restored old building housed Ostlers restaurant, where you could always have a savoury crockpot. Situated in historic Spon Street, the building was centuries old and had "wonderfully uneven floors, fantastic crockpots sampled more than once on a Saturday lunchtime" by budding gastronome Sue Lowe.

But it had something else that wasn't on the menu - a ghost named George! He was blamed for unusual happenings: "Stock flying from shelves, glasses being smashed, and stones being thrown at a customer", reports Sue. George was perhaps annoyed by this invasion of his privacy by hungry Dirty Stop Outs!

Jules Little and his friends enjoyed going to

Fishy Moores for fish and chips after their roller skating sessions at Coventry Sports Centre. But they dropped that habit in their late teens. 'We had grown up and our rituals did as well, at Fishy Moore's expense! It was the pub for us after skating."

For those who loved to eat their greens, the opening of Herbs in 1982 made a very welcome change. It offered a range of tasty meat-free dishes in a nice atmosphere and went on to win an Egon Ronay award.

Lesley Jackson who co-ran the restaurant with brother Robert and business partner Richard Davis said:

"We've done for vegetarianism what Danny la Rue has done for drag."

Popular nightspot the Dog and Trumpet was also known for its hearty, hot lunches. Early in the decade it got the nickname the Lanchester Poly's common room as so many students went there for

A crockpot and a ghost called George at Ostlers on Spon Street!

cheap 'traditional fare' and 'fresh produce', with main courses from £1.70. People flocked there for a good feed when times were hard or even when they were good!

Over at the Belgrade Theatre, the Stagebite café was popular and not just with theatre-goers for coffees and meals. Students with big appetites but small budgets found they could be well-fed in the first-floor café that had a cowboy/western theme

including red and white checked tablecloths. One of the best value meals was the "One-Man Show"- a beefburger, salad and bread for £2.

Warwick University student newspaper the Boar was scathing about Coventry's eateries. Their advice to students who had hunger pangs when in the city? Get on the bus and head back to campus. *"An enormous amount of courage and an iron constitution are required for eating out in Coventry,"* the paper wrote.

It recommended that those who were "desperate, and boy you'd have to be, the obvious place to risk is the Wimpy." There were several Wimpy Bars dotted around the centre offering a quick, cheap meals. This included the iconic Round Café in the Lower Precinct. They recommended this for those "whose speciality is goldfish impressions!"

There was also Coventry's own version of the Wimpy, Mr. Big, whose beefburgers in the view of the Boar newspaper were "a damn sight worse!"

Coventry council renewed its efforts to offer civic catering at the start of the eighties. They ran the Bridge Restaurant, Hertford Grill and the Sports Centre cafeteria plus some smaller snack bars and outlets. The idea was that, "Whether you fancy a choc-ice in a Coventry park or a slap-up meal in a plush city-centre restaurant, the city council's catering department can oblige."

The problem was that running costs were high so many of their establishments lost money. Efforts were made to attract 'businessmen' but Coventry's declining economic situation meant there were fewer of those around.

Optimistic councillor Waugh said in 1980 that, 'like the city itself, the catering department will rise from the ashes. There is no shadow of doubt in our minds that it will get back into profit. Why else is the private sector screaming at us to sell?"

Unfortunately, things only got worse. The Hertford Grill closed down not long after.

Others followed as the decade progressed paving the way for chains such as McDonalds to grab key sites in the city.

Belgrade Theatre with first floor Stagebite café

Cheering crowds waiting for the FA Cup victory bus

Fans celebrating by the elephant   **Front Cover of Radio Times**

SKY BLUE HEAVEN! COVENTRY CITY LIFT THE FA CUP AND THE CITY

CHAPTER 6

Maxine Smyth and family waiting outside the Newlands for mini bus to Wembley

Inset: Coventry's Owen Owen Department store getting behind the Sky Blues

Imagine today's football players finding sixpence in their boots if they won a match! That's what happened back in the late 19th century if Singers FC were victorious. Willie Stanley, an employee of local cycle firm Singers, set up the team in 1883. It very soon became Coventry City FC.

Over their long history, the Sky Blues never won much. But that changed dramatically on May 16th, 1987 when they lifted the FA Cup at Wembley and the whole city with it. The team were the underdogs against Tottenham Hotspurs and a certain Mr Jimmy Greaves said he'd eat his hat if they won.

The Sky Blues won 3-2 after extra time with much chanting of "eat yer hat, Jimmy!" The whole city went ballistic with joy!

The Road to Wembley
CCFC was languishing in the doldrums of the Third Division in 1961. Former Fulham player Jimmy Hill comes along like a knight in shining football kit and things start to change. He gave the club a good shake-up that led to promotions and ultimately that much-prized piece of silverware.

They won the Division Two title in 1966–67 and entered the First Division at last. Londoner Jimmy Hill became Coventry's very own football legend. The Sky Blue image is largely down to him and the change of kit brought about a renewed sense of identity. He looked at conditions for fans as well as players and made some improvements there too.

Mr Hill also helped to pen the club's song, Play Up Sky Blues, which could be heard right across

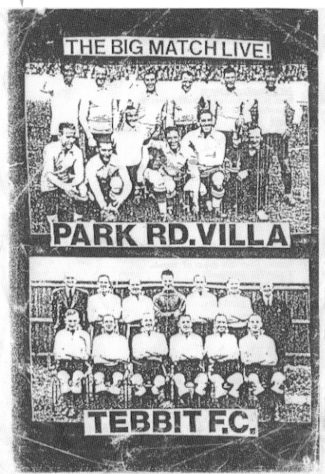

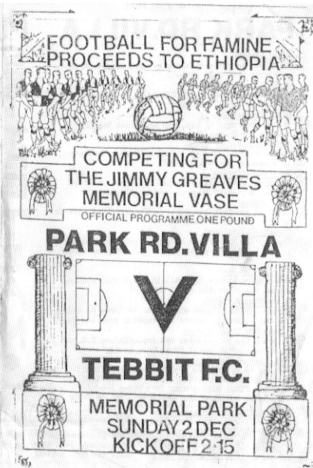

Coventry's Council House all decked up in Sky Blue surrounded by cheering crowds

Wembley and Coventry on that super Saturday in 1987. After leaving Coventry in 1967, Hill kept close links with the club and the city, returning as chairman in 1980.

Gillian Dawson: "I was living in London so got the train to Coventry to watch the game with my mates. The train broke down but made it back and we saw the match in the Gosford Park pub. We were all hokey-cokeying around the pub at full time. Fantastic weekend!"

The 'Sky Blue revolution' was felt everywhere, with the feel-good factor of the club's rise spilling over into the city's industry. Car production seemed to go up when the Sky Blues did well according to academic Andrew Dawes. Fans felt a sense of local pride and put that little bit extra in when back at work on Monday mornings.

Coventry's 1986/87 cup run was going so well that even those not keen on football got involved. Arnold William had never been to a football match before but went to the semi-final against Leeds at Sheffield's Hillsborough ground.

"It was amazing, even though I saw little of the game through the sardine-packed crowd. I am not a games person but the excitement and patriotism of watching Coventry rise up to be serious cup contenders infected even me. No other sporting occasion has ever enthused me enough to feel that I wanted to feel part of it by being a spectator."

Meryl Barrett:"I remember my mum who worked in the Council House being allowed to go inside to watch the victory parade. Myself and family went instead of her as she didn't want to go!"

City fan Nick Edgington was elated at the 3-2 win, but perturbed by the some actions of the police against a crowd that was "doing nothing." Two years later Hillsborough became the scene of tragedy when 96 supporters died.

The Sky Blues beat Liverpool in a League game on May 2nd, surely a sign of what was to come. In the week before the big game, excitement built and the local paper ran daily features with information, competitions and tips about how best to watch the game.

Tom Jarvis: "Mercia radio commentary was I believe instrumental in Coventry City FC's winning of the FA Cup in '87! It was all part of the atmosphere they helped to foster."

The general feeling was that, win, draw or lose, we'd won. Just reaching the FA final was such a fantastic achievement, no matter what the final score was on the day itself.

Coventry's Cup Final squad recorded Go For It City to mark the occasion, which got to number 61 in the charts. It was played and heard all over the city during this exciting time.

Sky Blues fan Bob Waggitt praises local SILK Disco DJ Jim Twyneham, 'the voice of Highfield Road,' as he was match day presenter. Jim had been spotted for the job at an awards night for a junior football team, when CCFC's co-manager George Curtis heard his distinctive voice. His first game as stadium announcer was in August 1986 and fans loved him.

Jim took his duties seriously and had a Sky Blues suit made, says Bob.

"Jim got the material from the CCFC shirt manufacturer and he asked the club's tailor to make it. SILK Disco sponsored my local team Finham Park Rangers and Jim, along with fellow SILK DJ Graham Wood, supported the team for many years throughout the 1970s and 1980s. They were good friends with many of the team from their early days and SILK often provided the disco at our functions."

It was all happening for City's goalkeeper Steve 'Oggy' Ogrizovic in the week before the big game. Being part of the FA Cup final squad was memorable in itself but wife Carolyn was about to have their second child. Carolyn opted to bring forward by a few days an inducement for the overdue baby. She didn't want Steve getting distracted on Cup Final day! Their daughter Rachel was born a few days before the big day.

Silk Disco DJ and 'voice of Highfield Road' Jim Twyneham in his Sky Blue suit making a presentation for Finham Park Rangers FC, July 1989

Employees at Remploy showing their Sky Blue colours!

Linda Keller's snap of Coventry's Council House during the Victory parade

The Big Day!

Saturday May 16th, 1987. CCFC had a date with Tottenham Hotspur and with history.

Many Dirty Stop Outs headed for Wembley or home for the game of the century. Nick Edgington had a precious ticket but nearly never made it to Wembley. Circumstances seemed to be against him, twice!

"I had to choose between the game and my mother's third wedding! She set the date months before. As the City kept winning, I started worrying. When they won the semi-final, everyone was asking what I was going to do. My wife was going to the final so I chose to go with her. I couldn't tell mum to her face so phoned her instead! I offered to go to the wedding in my Sky Blue kit on the way

Maxine Smyth's dad complete with sky blue beard on Cup Final day

to the station. But mum didn't want me standing there looking at my watch getting impatient."

Nick's mum had people wandering off at the reception to watch the game. On the way to the final, Nick had transport issues.

"We were on the last train from Coventry to Wembley that morning. It was delayed and we missed the start. Got to our seats just as Spurs scored. Not happy! But a great day in the end."

When the elated Nick got home that night, he saw that the video tape he'd put in to record the match had ran out before the end, due to extra time being played.

Maxine Smyth found out she'd be Wembley-bound the night before.

"My cousin got us tickets on the black market. He must have paid well over the odds but gave us them as a wedding present. My brother's mate was taking a mini bus and had two seats left. So, we were lucky and were on our way to Wembley!

"We left at 7.30am and we're outside Wembley at 10.30am. The atmosphere was amazing and so was the whole day."

Maxine Smyth: "I'd love a time machine to go back and do it all again."

Those in town on match day morning would have seen people hurrying to do their shopping before heading home. Many shops and market stalls closed early: no point in staying open when everyone was going to be glued to the telly.

By mid-afternoon, an eerie hush descended and the deserted city had a 'ghost town' feel. But this time for a very good reason!

Maurice Burnell watched the final at Coventry's Walsgrave Hospital's maternity unit.

"We were all cheering and booing and when that last goal went in we jumped off our seats. I was nearly in tears and couldn't bear to watch. We kept saying 'Blow the whistle ref, please!'"

Down in Sussex, Sue Long was the only Coventry supporter for miles around and threw herself into the occasion.

"I got my Sky Blue stuff on, dressed up the dog and children, the scarf was over the TV as I watched the match at a friend's house. I drove back to Chichester afterwards with my scarf flying from my car window, hooting my horn to bemused passers by! Then a wonderful person turned up at my house with a sky blue decorated cake and some fizz so we toasted that famous victory in style. I may have missed all the camaraderie and craziness that went on in Coventry, but I turned my little corner of England sky blue that wonderful day!"

Stuart Beamish: "When you came out of Wembley there were stalls festooned with Tottenham Hotspur FA CUP Winners 1987 scarves and t-shirts. Laugh? I nearly bought one. One guy was banging out Coventry ones as fast as he could."

The Cup Final victory brought a sound to the city that hadn't been heard for 100 years - Coventry Cathedral's bells! They had been restored and were due to be rung later that month but the Provost thought, what the heck, let's ring them now!

Sue Lowe plus doggie supporting the Sky Blues and left - It's all gone Sky Blue! Sue Lowe's house on Cup Final day

Philip Sephton: "I remember after getting back to Coventry from Wembley all the city centre pubs were locked, full to the rafters! Amazingly we managed to get in to the Town Wall tavern to celebrate. Great memories!"

Sue Lowe's 14 year-old nephew Derek from Doncaster was a Sky Blues fan. He travelled from Coventry to Wembley in the care of her friends, including one with sky blue highlights in her hair!

"We won! Everybody rushed out, yelling. Amazing! Switch to 2am and much celebrating later. Still no sign of Derek or our friends, so we went into the city to look for him."

Sue will never forget the sights and sounds that night as crowds celebrated wildly.

"The noise was phenomenal with all the cars going by, horns blasting. I don't think I'll ever forget the sight of people hanging off the Coventry Evening Telegraph balcony, others jumping, and landing, usually unceremoniously, on the cars driving past including a Porsche, its suspension never being the same I bet!"

Derek was eventually found back at their local, the Herald, around 4am. "A night to remember, forever!"

Far left: Sky Blues fan Phil Sephton gets his hands on the FA Cup at a charity event, late 1987

DJ Jules Little: *"The best night ever! The city celebrated like never before. Go For it City was played every other record. The population of this sky blue paradise walked around the city centre admiring the sky blue fountains outside the Belgrade Theatre. Total strangers hugged in unbridled joy. One old gent I started talking to at around four in the morning said 'It wasn't this good when we won the war!'"*

Bringing the Cup home! Victory parade

When the team brought the FA Cup home the next day, an estimated quarter of a million people flocked into the city and lined the route to greet the squad and catch a glimpse of the Cup. Sarah Soden stood on top of a bank to watch the parade along with many others. Some clambered onto buses, some even onto the Cathedral!

Maxine Smyth bagged a great spot.

"I took pics from the top of Broadgate House which Coventry City Council Council opened up for us. Many businesses and offices opened their doors to their staff that day. Such a great atmosphere in the city!"

Dogs were not left out! Nick Edgington and his wife had a cute, sky blue scarf-wearing dog with them. "We went to the Rising Sun in Spon Street afterwards and lots of people played with him."

Pete Clemons: *"Coventry had the best and worst of times during the eighties. They won the FA Cup then lost the Charity Shield weeks later. Each result ended in a Dirty Stop Outs night!"*

Fans gathering for CCFC bus parade

CCFC victory parade bus

The victory bus visited Walsgrave hospital where goalie Steve Ogrizovic's wife and new-born baby were. It was a real tonic for everyone there though they had to keep the visit a secret!

Sue Lowe recalls a celebratory cocktail at Ray's Bar in the Leofric Hotel. "'Blue Heaven'- gorgeous! It captured the Sky Blues victory perfectly." Stuart Beamish liked Ray's usual 'Sky Blue Special', which he and his mates would sup after a win (or a loss.)

"Ray wouldn't say what was in this prize winning cocktail. He kept the recipe to himself."

The Sky Blue team were heroes, not just goal scorers Dave Bennett and Keith Houchen. The latter's goal was voted Goal of the Season. Cyrille Regis, squad member from 1984 to 1991, helped to lift the Cup. His winning ways on and off the pitch endeared him to fans and Cyrille did much to address issues of racism in the game and encourage other black players.

The CCFC squad led by John Sillett and George Curtis found a place in the history books and Coventry peoples' hearts on that memorable day. Let's all sing together- play up Sky Blues!

The victorious team greeted by ecstatic crowds

Nick Edgington's cup final train ticket, precious FA Cup Ticket and victory commemoration mugs

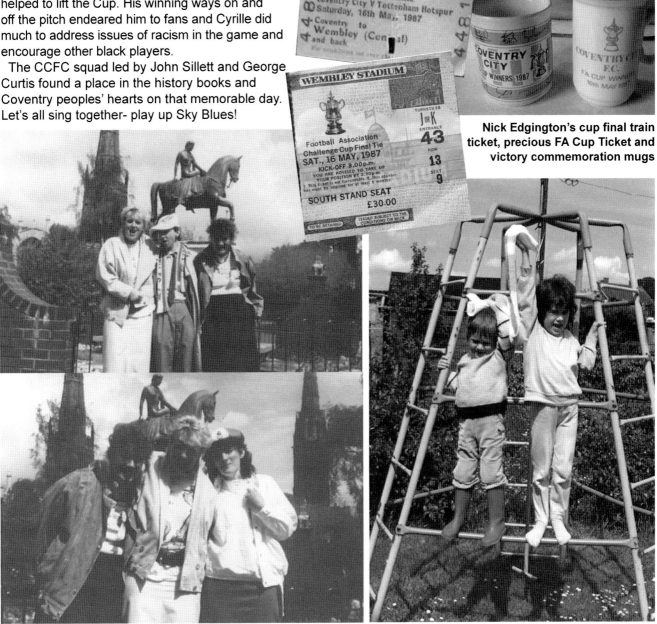

Sky Blues fan Philip Sephton and friends in front of Coventry's Lady Godiva

Sue Lowe's kids all dressed up for Sky Blue's big day

Lesley Hannah Murray "Crikey - I was in that crowd with my dad!"

THE WEDGE CAFE - CAMPAIGNS, BOOKS AND HOW TO MAKE A FANZINE

The Wedge bookshop and cafe on the High Street

Y ou couldn't find a place more aptly named than the Wedge bookshop and café on Coventry's High Street. Trev Teasdel remembers it literally as a tall thin building wedged between two bigger buildings.

Sue Lowe says it was all a bit higgledy-piggledy, like a rabbit warren, but a really good place and a bit radical. Ray Jenkins, another Wedge fan agrees. "It was a great place to meet up and share a view over a coffee. Everyone knew each other."

The Wedge became the place to find out about demos, gigs, CND rallies, political meetings, women's groups and benefit rights.

Its notice board was always packed with information and tables overflowed with leaflets and flyers. It was also where folks could pick up a fanzine or two and discuss politics at length.

Clare Allington-Dixon: *"I spent so many childhood years there with my mum. Great place, great books, great food. Seem to remember it was definitely full of punks, commies and skinheads or my mum wouldn't have been in there! And definitely good coffee and fags."*

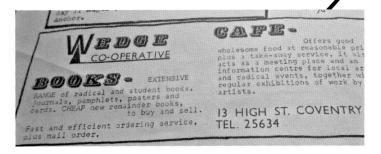

Coventry and the concrete jungle

PROTEST AND SURVIVE

March & Rally, Sunday October 26th
Assemble 11am Hyde Park / Rally 2-30pm Trafalgar Square

live music from THE SPECIALS
and THE POP GROUP

COACHES FROM UNIVERSITY, COVENTRY AND LEAMINGTON

FOR CND INFORMATION SEE JEREMY BOWEN (C/O GERMAN DEPT
DAVE JOHNSON 045 ROUTES

Punk band TDA playing at CND gig under the flyover

The label 'alternative' was heard a lot in the 1980s, with campaigns for this and against that. This small café played a big role as jobs became scarce and money too tight to mention.

Gillian Dawson: "Spent many hours in the Wedge, the sort of place that never changed. I remember it in the very early days with long benches. It was definitely easier to get chatting to people, always lots of debate."

Run by a group of former students, the aim was not only to feed the masses but also to let them know about all sorts of campaigns. As unemployment in the city rose, there was a mission to arm the citizens with information about their rights and where to go for help. Also how to help themselves through starting co-ops and campaigns.

All of this activism created big appetites. The Wedge served up tasty vegetarian food at a time when being veggie wasn't easy.

The staff got to know the customers who would pop in for a browse and a chat, sometimes just when they were thinking of closing up! Nigel Williams worked at Wedge between 1978 - 87 and was a member of the co-operative.

"I remember a certain Rich Mulligan liked coming to the bookshop about ten to five on a Saturday. Typical! Just when I was thinking of closing up to go over the road to the Rose and Crown, to read all the pamphlets, very slowly!"

But as Nigel knew Rich, a regular, he really didn't mind. Rich was a veritable punk activist back then

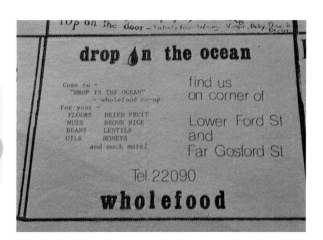

and recalls the Wedge being a punk-friendly place at a time when other places weren't.

"The Wedge! A legendary café and book shop, long before hipster bookshops sold coffee."

The Wedge was popular with feminists and anti-nuclear campaigners. Supporting the miner's strike (1984-85) was also another cause that customers adopted with fund-raisers and demos.

Very often these activities would involve gigs such as the CND one under the ring road flyover in 1982. Anne Porter was there and remembers local bands performing, like punk outfit TDA, just getting on stage and playing. It was all a bit free and easy by the sounds of it!

All of this activism created big appetites. The Wedge served up tasty vegetarian food at a time when being a veggie wasn't easy. Sue Lowe licks her lips when casting her mind back to meals she had there.

"The wonderful café served an amazing selection of dishes, including spicy spinach and chickpea soup, and butterbean and coriander salad. I was doing an Open University degree in the 1980s and also bought a few books from there."

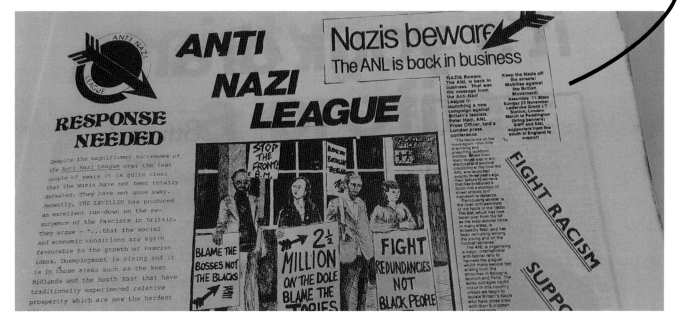

Above: What Trev bought from The Wedge

1st issue of Coventry's fanzine produced by Martin Bowes and issue 7

People flocked there for the legendary kidney bean flan and if the main dishes weren't to their taste, hot jacket potatoes were always available. Non-veggies were also catered for. With the Wedge being located just down the road from the Poly, students would queue there at lunchtimes alongside shop and office workers.

The best thing on the menu for Carolyn Tracey Tomkins was granary bread with cream cheese, fresh orange slices and cashew nuts. She's still making and eating this combo today!

The café also had links to Drop in the Ocean, an independent health food shop in the City Arcade. Wedge staff member Nigel Williams remembers this link.

"We started off getting the bread from Drop in the Ocean as well as other stuff, like lentils and herbs."

Drop in the Ocean caused Sue Lowe to do a fair bit of drooling.

"There was always at least one plate of freshly-baked flapjacks, pies, cakes or biscuits, in the glass cabinet at the front of the shop. Very tempting, amongst all the vitamins and supplements!"

Students saved many pennies at the bookshop, buying second hand. Some lecturers even sent them there to buy the set texts rather than the mainstream bookshops.

And sometimes romance was in the air as well. Jon met a German exchange student, Ingrid, when he worked there during the eighties. They drifted apart once she had returned home and it was many years later when they were reunited thanks to the wonders of the internet. They married in 2007.

The Wedge team played an important role in setting up Coventry News, an alternative newspaper, which started late 1970s and continued through the early 1980s. Trev Teasdel went to the first meeting at the Wedge and remembers staff there initiating it along with Arol who had worked on the Broadgate Gnome in the 1970s.

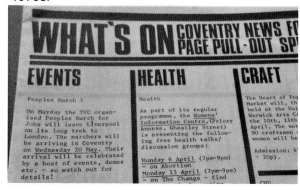

Trev Teasdel: *"I used to pick up copies of Coventry News in the 1980s. I think they all must have re-mortgaged their houses to open the Wedge!"*

Coventry News was packed with information about what was going on in the city, benefits advice, political gatherings and more. It fitted into the Wedge's philosophy, as did Alternative Sounds, Coventry's very own fanzine, which the Wedge stocked.

Alternative Sounds was the brainchild of Coventry music fan Martin Bowes whose discovery of punk in 1977 "totally changed" his life. He was inspired by the music, politics and "do-it yourself attitude". Fanzines were part of all that and he read many that were springing up across the country. But Coventry lacked its own which he thought was odd given the great music scene.

What was to be done? Produce one yourself, of course! All part of that do-it-yourself approach. Martin talked about the idea to Dill of God's Toys and they made it happen. Armed with information about bands and gigs, an issue was produced in 1979, which they touted around local record shops and 'alternative' venues such as the Wedge.

Financed out of their dole money, the first 100 copies sold out quickly even though somewhat rough and ready. More copies were produced and a successful bid to the Prince's Trust brought in a grant of £100 so that the fanzine could be printed properly.

At its peak, the fanzine reached 1000 copies. The Lanch's Student Union was involved in printing some of the issues until a bit of controversy about an image of a Page 3 girl with a severed head. That was the end of that collaboration. Martin says that people misunderstood what he was trying to do with this image, or "maybe I just didn't get it right. I was about 19 at the time." His attempt to make an anti-sexist statement backfired.

Between 1979-1981,18 issues of the fanzine were produced. It helped pave the way for other local fanzines like Adventures in Reality, which Nick Edgington used to pop into the Wedge to buy, as well as Alternative Sounds.

When Prince Charles met with some beneficiaries of his Trust's grants in Birmingham, Martin was there and the local press referred to it as the 'Prince and the punk' encounter!

Paul Hookham went to school with Martin's youngest brother. "There was always fresh 45s to listen to on a Thursday. The issues of Alternative Sounds were always looked forward to. Martin was a true champion of Coventry's music scene and a gent."

Pete Chambers believes that the early eighties

Martin Bowes (centre) founder of fanzine Alternative Sounds meets Prince Charles, 1980

Fanzine founder Martin Bowes invite to meet Prince Charles, 1980

Prince and the punk rock image

UNK gear worn by three young Coventry magazine producers, caught the attention of Prince Charles in Birmingham yesterday.

The Prince was highly amused by their outrageous gear, said the 21-year-old magazine editor, Martin Bowes, of 143, Moat Avenue, Green Lane.

And he thought the red hair and dog collar sported by the magazine assistants, Robert Lapworth and Julie Giblock "very funny."

Martin was able to thank Prince Charles for the £100 from the Prince's Trust charity which helped the alternative pop music ...

In ... with ...

THE PRINCE'S TRUST

THIS PERMIT WILL ADMIT THE BEARER INTO THE SMALL HEATH SCHOOL AND COMMUNITY CENTRE MUNTZ STREET, BIRMINGHAM 10 ON FRIDAY 30th MAY, 1980 VALID UNTIL 2p.m. ONLY

Press cutting of when the Prince met a punk Martin Bowes!

music scene really benefited from Alternative Sounds. It was more than just a fanzine: it really helped bands and the city as a whole as the music scene grew and attracted more attention.

Pete also has a few interesting things to point out!

"In Issue 3, Martin published an exclusive Specials tour diary hand written by Jerry Dammers. Instead of just photocopying it, he wrote it out by hand and threw the originals away. Just how collectable would they have been today?"

Martin Bowes gained useful experience from it (perhaps not to throw away hand written diaries!) and it gave him access to venues such as the Coventry Theatre to interview bands. He too believes it helped the local music scene to grow and made an impact.

The Sent from Coventry album, featuring local bands, also came out of this fanzine and was another of Martin's initiatives. Released in May 1980, it had a special copy of the fanzine inside. It also had a picture of the Wedge on its cover along with other Coventry scenes.

Martin was then invited by the BBC to explain 'How to make a fanzine' as part of its Something Else series. The show was very youth oriented

Taking a lunch break in the small park between Hay Lane and Pepper Lane

chi
bar

chi
bar

THE MUCH TALKED ABOUT...

**CLOSING DOWN
PARTY FOR
WEDGE.**

TO BE HELD AT THE WEST INDIAN CLUB
SPON STREET,
ON SATURDAY THE 1st NOVEMBER

DOORS OPEN 9 PM. DOORS CLOSE 11.15

LATE BAR / FOOD .
RAFFLE OF WEDGE
MEMORABILIA .
DJs / BANDS . ENTERTAINMENT .

DONATIONS GRATEFULLY RECEIVED ON THE NIGHT
TO COVER EXPENSES.
INVITATION ONLY , VIA WEDGE
ADMITS ONE
PLEASE BRING YOUR INVITE TO THE DOOR
AND BE SURE YOU HAVE ONE EACH.

The Wedge then and now

Martin being filmed at General Wolfe for Something Else programme

How to make a fanzine! BBC Something Else programme with Martin Bowes and Dill of God's Toys, 1980

and went to different cities to talk to young people about what they were doing in their local community. It was filmed in a house in Dorset Road and at the music pub the General Wolfe. Dill and God's Toys featured in it as well as they were instrumental in helping to launch the Alternative Sounds fanzine.

Dominic Mangan would pick up his copy of another fanzine in Wedge, Ded Yampy, which he describes as something like a rag mag and punk fanzine. There also a band by the same name run by local Pete Pallanick's band. Rich Mulligan remembers Pete as "a local character, one of many. A big tall bloke with rockabilly hair cut who wore a dressing gown sometimes around town."

Gillian Dawson thinks the Wedge was one of the longest running co-ops before it closed down.

"Some of the co-op members left and those

remaining ran out of steam together with the increasing financial problems running an independent bookshop. Gutted at the time but a great party at the end. Won something in the raffle but no idea what!"

Arnold William: "Its popularity as a meeting place for extended conversation over one cup of tea probably was one of the reasons it became uneconomic and I think they couldn't afford the cost of building work to comply with Council Legislation."

The Wedge kept going until the 1990s before finally succumbing to financial and building issues. The days of radical books, fanzines and fags over a leisurely coffee or healthy lunch came to an end.

Punk fashion

Riddy's army surplus next to Sweeney Todd the barbers

An older pic of Riddy's Surplus Stores in Gosford Street

Small in-
dependent
shops in the
City Arcade

Inset: The
birdcage

SHOULDER PADS, PERMS AND ARMY SURPLUS:
GETTING THE LOOK JUST RIGHT!

CHAPTER 8

Phil Rooney reckons his worst fashion mistake was wearing dungarees to raves. His best look was being suited 'n' booted.

"I loved to get a suit and tie on to go to Park Lane and the Pink Parrot."

Clare Allington had a dungaree fashion faux pas but her highest point was an exotic lycra catsuit. Make up and accessorizing was important whichever style people were aiming for.

Fashions in the 1980s veered from practical demo-wear: big boots, berets and boiler suits, to the utterly frivolous ra-ra skirts. Army surplus stores were frequently raided for basic items at low prices.

Did we wear them well? Dirty Stops Outs all tried hard to get the look right, whether they opted to be new romantics, Adam Ant look-a-likes or punks with pink mohicans.

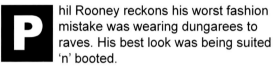

> **Liz Smith:** *"I had a white boiler suit, I rolled the bottoms up so they were above my ankles, big belt, chunky jewellery and topped off with four inch white stilettos! I felt amazing. One of my friends asked if I'd been decorating!"*

Some went for the rolled up sleeves look, just because stars like Don Johnson in Miami Vice did. That's the view of Sue Lowe.

"I had a lovely charcoal grey seersucker jacket that conveniently came with the sleeves already rolled up! It also had massive should pads. All very Miami Vice."

Many referred to it as 'power dressing' and Sue took that very seriously, wearing said outfit to a job interview.

"I was asked, in a condescending tone, if I got taken seriously in IT what with being an ex-secretary. Non-PC comments like that were pretty much par for the course back then. I replied with a smile, 'not until now, no.'"

Sue then stood up, tossed her frosted hair back and sashayed out leaving the interviewers gobsmacked.

She says it was one of her finest moments!

So, what people wore was not just about how they wanted to look but how they wanted to be treated as well. And this worked both ways as Mark Rewhorn discovered. He was the recipient of a special tie from a girlfriend, decorated with small pigs: the male chauvinist pig tie!

"I can't remember which disgruntled former girlfriend bought it for me, or what my particular crime for earning it was. No doubt I truly deserved it!"

Hunting out 'that look'- from C&A to the Shambles

Many fashion shoppers began their clothes hunt in the Lower Precinct at C&A. There was variety on offer at reasonable prices whether people wanted work wear, casual clothes or something for parties or dancing the night away.

All the usual suspects were to be found in the shopping precinct: M&S (still Marks and Spencers then!) British Home Stores and department store Owen Owen. The latter was a bit more pricey but good for that special occasion. Smaller fashion shops included Van Allen, Richards, Werff, Hammells and Wallis.

Men were well catered for at places like Nickelby's, Fosters and Burtons. Mark Rewhorn liked to wear flared jeans, with a crease in them. He shudders at the thought now but he was so serious about getting the crease razor sharp that he used a Pifco electric trouser press!

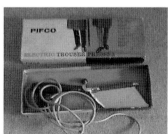 

Needed to get that perfect crease! MarkRewhorn's Pifco electric trouser press and his Chauvinist Pig tie- a present from a disgruntled girlfriend!

Wonder what Peeping Tom made of all these shops and shoppers?

Rooftop parking on Coventry's market

Shopping central! Centre of the Precinct with C&A in the distance

Laurence Benjamin Arnold: "I started out with army surplus, you could say Riddy's was my tailor, a proper army surplus store in Far Gosford Street. You could buy almost anything there. They used to have a brass diving helmet in the window, though I'm not sure if it was actually for sale. As the decade wore on I gravitated towards the country look - Barbour jacket and moleskin trousers - no moles were harmed in the process!"

Far Gosford Street was popular for its second hand shops where fashionable bargains could be found. Lyn Farnell remembers one called Jeans very well as it's where her husband bought the suit he got married in and also one of the bridesmaids dresses! Carole Tracey Tomkins was another fan of this shop. She and a friend bought mini dresses from there when they went to see Diana Ross at the NEC in Birmingham in the early eighties.
Nick Edgington

bought his three-button narrow lapel jacket for 2 Tone gigs from a Far Gosford Street second hand shop, getting a lot of wear out of it.

"I remember buying a full length tweed overcoat for my 'long coat look', and wearing it with Docs on Blackpool beach. There was a brief time when Kid Creole inspired a zoot suit revival so I bought a suit and a jacket, with padded shoulders and huge lapels. I wore those to gigs at the Wolfe, Busters and the Pink Parrot. And for my New Romantic look, I bought a Tyrolean hunting jacket, looking a bit like a Beatles Nehru jacket but with horn buttons and embroidered lapels. I remember wearing that that to the Human League at Tiff's."

Nick was also an army surplus store raider and personalised a dull green jumper, in a colourful way. He made a corporal's chevron from five small badges with the following words: Ian Dury, Sex, Drugs, Rock, Roll. He thought it looked cool, anyway!

Martin Corne had a pair of German moleskins.

"They must have been for a very short-legged person, but on me were above ankle height. Absolutely loved them. Also my Velvet Underground T-shirt. I got it from a small printers up Moor Street or Providence Street in Earlsdon."

Nick Edgington: "Me and two friends bought ex-Canadian Army officers trench coats and I wore a trilby. When we walked into a pub carrying our pool cues, someone called out 'bloody hell! It's the Mafia!"

Far left: Martin Corne wore his German moleskins to go back packing around France!

Coventry's pedestrian shopping precinct

Upper Precinct featuring BHS, Marks and Spencer and Saxone shoe shop

Intershop - everything under one roof!

Sue Lowe remembers two places where small independent traders were all under one roof: Intershop, next to Bull Yard, and the Shambles. Intershop was originally set up as a co-operative by 20 leaseholders and was at its peak of popularity in the 1980s.

The Shambles, opposite the Coventry Theatre in Hales Street, was a small indoor market. Phil Rooney recalls it as "a place of legends", with dungarees, fake sovereign rings and breakfasts. Leigh Torrance also remembers the "great cafe at the back."

It was also a good place to get your ears pierced, though for Alan West, both times he did that his ears resembled space hoppers. Clearly, the first space hopper experience didn't deter him from going back for more! Sid Wilson got his ear pierced in the Shambles at the tender age of ten and lived to tell the tale.

> **Sue Lowe:** *"The Shambles Arcade and Intershop were both well worth a browse on a Saturday morning, with everything under one roof. You could get your ears pierced and have a cup of coffee."*

Coventry's circular indoor market remained shopper's paradise with bargains to be had on the many stalls. Stuart Beamish's entire wardrobe was supplied by one market stall - Deakins.

It was all the rage to wear brightly coloured tights and you could usually find a pair to match your outfit in the market. Shocking pink, yellow, lime green legs were all popular and there was always an occasion calling for fishnets, especially for men aiming to get the St. Trinian's look just right.

A nice little independent for 'original clothes' could be found in The Burges-Revive. It catered for those seeking something a little different but not at stupid prices! It was also community-minded and took part in a fashion show fundraiser at the Dog and Trumpet in July 1989.

Shop owner Mike McHugh was very pleased with the way the event went and the amount raised, £250, which went to help the work of Coventry's Community Drugs team. One of the city's top hair salons, Beepers, was also involved in this fashion fundraiser.

The 1980s saw people generally relieved to step down from their vertigo-inducing platforms of the previous decade to more sensible footwear - sometimes anyway! A favourite style for women early in the decade was the pixie boot in a variety of colours.

> **Louise Cherry:** *"I loved my bright blue pixie boots! I often wore blue tights to match."*

Doc Martens were the sensible option for demos or just stomping around town or the dance floor. Though often associated with skinheads, many people wore them. They received a boost when local band King adopted them as part of their look.

Manager Perry Haines had set out to create a distinctive image for King, which included Docs. The band emphasized they weren't a symbol of 'aggro' and painted their boots different colours. This became part of their brand image. King members were presented with the new design the 20-hole version, which they wore at the debut gig at London's Dominion Theatre in 1984.

Many teenaged fans followed suit. DJ Jules Little was one of these, mad about King, but a bit too scared of his mum to paint his boots!

For lesser mortals who didn't get free Docs, Dolcis shoe shop remained a firm favourite. Barratts and Mansfield's also competed for shoe shopper's attention.

Dotted around the city centre were some post-war prefab shops, hardly looking out of place. Erected on a temporary basis after the massive damage of the war, they just stayed put and were still trading in the 1980s. The PDSA charity shop was one on Corporation Street and others could be found at Broadgate.

Nick Edgington always loved his Doc Martens!

Postwar prefab shops still alive and well in Corporation Street in 1980s

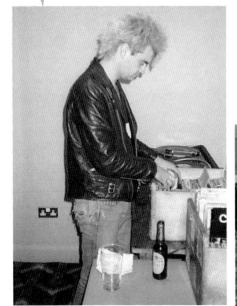

DJ Rich Mulligan's 1980s look- jeans and leather jacket

Waiting for buses in Broadgate- 'top' of the town

Working that 80s cool look- Steve Guest

Having your hair done - a real headache!

How many women have painful memories of the hairdresser in the 1980s?

The frosted highlight look involved a powdered rubber cap and crochet hook to drag strands of hair through. Sue Lowe cringes at the thought.

"I still remember that it could feel painful having those strands dragged through! And of course there is always a time when it goes horribly wrong. The attractive blonde look I was aiming for once ended up having an unfortunate greenish hue. Not a great look!"

Sue had a friend who supported the Sky Blues during their successful 1987 FA Cup campaign in her own special way.

"One of my best friends, an avid City fan, believed that 'having her hair done' on the day of each cup game was a good thing because City won. Being blonde with 'big' hair, she vowed she'd have sky blue highlights if they got to the final. They did, she did, and they won!"

When in need of a hair-do, many Dirty Stop Outs headed for Paul's in Broadgate House or at Cannon Park and there was also Jayne at the Leofric. One favourite was Beepers salon.

Make-up rounded off any good fashion statement, including for male Dirty Stop Outs. It had to be dramatic in Sue Lowe's view, to go with that huge hair, shoulder pads and the rest.

People were also heavily influenced by the pop videos that really came into their own with MTV hitting our screens in the early eighties. Pop stars such as Annie Lennox and many others went big-time for a dramatic look, which many aspired to replicate.

Colours went into another dimension with eyes all sorts of weird and wonderful shades and eyebrows shaped in ways that made us look like relatives of Mr Spock on Star Trek. Sales of mascara and eye-liner probably went up, massively, and if your mum said 'take that muck off your face,' you probably didn't.

Just as music and Doc Martens had become multi-tone in 1980s Coventry, so did our make-up to finish off that 'special' look!

MOVING INTO MULTI-TONE AND COVENTRY BANDS PLAY FOR AFRICA

Just when people started to think Coventry's musical reign was over, along came King to claim the crown. Pete Chambers believes this was one of the city's favourite bands. Emerging out of the disbanded Reluctant Stereotypes, Paul King, Tony Wall and Colin Heanes first got together with several other musicians to form Raw Screens. From this outfit came the ground-breaking King.

With Perry Haines as their manager, success was always on the cards but it wasn't exactly overnight! Haines was founder of ID Magazine and video editor for top bands like Duran Duran. He had been very impressed by Paul King when he saw him with the Reluctant Stereotypes.

King's vocalist Paul King in action, Highfield Road football ground, September 1984

Pete Chambers remembers their promotional package that claimed King would take Coventry from 2 Tone to multi-tone. Early gigs in the city included the Hope and Anchor, the Dog and Trumpet and General Wolfe.

Pete Chambers: *"In Paul King they had a front man of the highest order: theatrical, good looking, charismatic with the perfect eighties voice."*

Signed by CBS, their first single Love and Pride was released in April 1984. It was love at first hearing for Jules Little who thought it was "bright, brash, catchy, infectious, technicolour music in a black and white world."

Thousands went out and bought it and, like Jules, had it glued to their record players. But it only reached Number 84. Second single Soul On My Boots, released that summer, didn't fare much better

Jules Little: *"In 1984 I was a teenager who'd discovered girls and pop music, both of which seemed out of reach. The former due to my ginger hair and acne, the latter as it was all good time music with videos shot in far flung places, a long way from a terraced house in Coventry. Then my neighbour played me a new single by a band called King, from Coventry, my town! The lead singer even attended the same school as me! The video wasn't in Rio but shot in a quarry with old oil drums and a wrecked car. This was instantly my music, my band."*

Steps in Time was released in December 1984. Jules and his gang repeatedly blasted it out on a cassette player in Coventry's Lower Precinct. Whether the late night Christmas shoppers appreciated that or not is another question!

But things were not going to plan chart-wise, so changes were made. After appearing on Channel 4's The Tube and playing support for Culture Club, things started to look up.

King's vocalist Paul King in action, Highfield Road football ground, September 1984

Their singles were re-released, faring much better in 1985.

King soon realised that younger fans were excluded from many venues due to the licensing laws. When they played at the Lanch they put on a special 3pm matinee, fixing the entrance fee at just 50p so teenagers could come along.

Jules Little went to Coventry City's Highfield Road football ground to see King's pre-testimonial match gig in September 1984. King did a 45 minute set before the match that was in honour of Sky Blue stalwart Brian Roberts. Jules left 15 minutes into the match. It was the band he had gone for, not the football!

He was elated to see the front page of the Coventry Evening Telegraph in February 1985, with the headline "They're 21 today!" King had broken into the charts big time and cracked open the champagne. It was a boost for the city, another great local band finding national success.

The Number One spot remained elusive, however, held onto by Elaine Paige and Barbara Dickson with I Know Him So Well, from the musical Chess. Jules Little still can't listen to that today. He's probably not the only one! He sums up nicely the link between fan and the band.

"Being a fan is special, being a fan of a local band is even better."

If 1985 was the year when King reigned, other Coventry stars shone brightly for famine relief in East Africa.

Cov Aid

In June 1985, Live Aid brought together the giants of the pop world, the strong desire to alleviate starvation in East Africa and Bob Geldoff's unique style of fundraising.

Many of those on the Coventry music scene decided they wanted to do something similar close to home. The result was a day-long concert at the Lanchester Poly on October 19th.

Pete Chambers: "Live Aid had an impact on us all, not least with the local music fraternity. Many had the idea of a local version of Live Aid and at the forefront was local soul legend and all-round good guy Ray King. He along with Coventry Evening Telegraph's music scribe Jim Taylor, the band This Heat, Lanch entertainments officer Dave Howarth and myself came together as the organising committee of what was christened Cov Aid. Mercia Sound and Coventry Cable TV came on board too."

Some useful publicity was generated by news that a local Page Three girl, Debee Ashby, was to appear as a 'guest.' Feminists at the Polytechnic were apparently incensed and planned to picket the concert with much column-space given to this story. But all publicity is good publicity and Pete tells us that it was all a set-up to promote the concert and sell tickets!

The local line-up for the day included Sheer Pride who have been described as a local band with a cool looking lead singer and very big haired guitarist. They were known for doing a great cover of the Cadburys Flake song, and throwing flakes into the crowd.

Also playing were Terminal Tears and This Heat. Headliners were local busking duo Jimmy Jimmy and Pauline Black's Supernaturals. And with Jerry Dammers as the event DJ, it was set to be very 'special' indeed.

Pete Chambers confirms that Cov Aid "represented the finest in local musical talent the City could muster."

Other local heroes were making appearances such as Coventry's top athletes David Moorcroft and Lorraine Baker. Local MP Dave Nellist, a former Lanch Poly and DJ, was also supporting the concert.

Bands played concurrently in the main hall and Biko Bar. Top of the bill was Colourfield who appeared on stage around 10.30 and entertained the audience with hits such as Castles In The Air, Colourfield and Thinking Of You. A great moment came when they were joined by Ian McCulloch of Echo and the Bunnymen, with an ad hoc version of the Doors' LA Woman thrilling the crowd!

Over 800 people attended Cov Aid, which was a huge success at many levels, including the sum of £4,425 that was raised.

Pete Chambers backstage pass for Cov Aid fundraising concert 1985

Sheer Pride

Terry Hall and Colourfield top the bill at Cov Aid fundraiser held at Coventry Polytechnic, 1985

Local band This Heat who performed at Cov Aid fundraiser 1985

COVAID
85
STARRING
FOR EAST AFRICA
COLOURFIELD
WITH
DESTINY — EUROPEAN SUN
INTIMATE OBSESSIONS — JIMMY JIMMY — JUMPIN' BAD
MAJOR 5 — RED ON RED — SHEER PRIDE
SPIDER MURPHY — STILL LIFE — THIS HEAT
TERMINAL TEARS — 20 DAYS — SUPERNATURALS
WITH LOCAL SPORTING AND POLITICAL CELEBRITIES
AT THE
LANCHESTER POLYTECHNIC
STUDENT UNION PRIORY ST COVENTRY CV1 3FJ
SATURDAY OCTOBER 19th 1985
DOORS OPEN 5.30 p.m. TICKETS — £1 FOR
ADMISSION PLUS £4 DONATION
TICKETS AVAILABLE FROM COV. POLY STUDENTS
UNION, COVENTRY EVENING TELEGRAPH OFFICES,
COVENTRY INFORMATION AND MERCIA SOUND.
TELEPHONE ENQUIRIES COV. 618961 and 442607
(12.00 to 2.00 p.m.)
IN CONJUNCTION WITH MERCIA SOUND, BRUM BEAT,
COVENTRY EVENING TELEGRAPH, COV POLY S.U.
AND COVENTRY CABLE TV.
R.O.A.R.

Debut single today for the Colourfield

Terminal Tears who appeared at the Cov Aid fundraiser in 1985

Indian flavour spices up star band's album

Primitives check out slow sales

THE KEY TO YOUR NEW HOME MAY BE JUST A FEW PAGES AWAY . . .

In tonight's Property Guide, starting on Page 24, a selection of the most beautiful new homes.

And Coventry was not done yet on the music front. Before the decade was out, another great band grabbed the headlines: the Primitives. Formed in the mid-1980s, vocalist Tracey Tracey and guitarist Paul Court were two constant members.

Local DJ Toby Davies sees the Primitives as "a genuine Cov band made up of people who were very much frequenters of local pubs and nightclubs such as the Rose and Crown, the Dog and Trumpet and Busters."

The 'Prims' as they were usually called were often labelled rather vaguely as an 'indie pop band'. The Coventry Evening Telegraph described their songs as "catchy and jangly." Their best-known hit Crash, released in 1988, became the soundtrack for the film Dumb and Dumber.

Other hits include Sick of It, Stop Killing Me and Out of Reach. Their single Really Stupid was voted by Mojo Magazine in 2008 as one of the Top 40 UK indie singles of all time - quite a claim to fame!

SICK OF IT!

Neville Hadsley meets Paul, Tracey and Tig of the new, assertive PRIMITIVES.

Kind of dancy

Rich Mulligan: "I once played Crash in Busters whilst Tracey the singer was actually up there. I seem to think she danced to it too."

One of their early songs was Lazy, the name of their own label. They usually recorded at Cabin

Studios on the London Road in Coventry. They later signed up for RCA records and released further singles, as well as re-recording some of their earlier material. Their first RCA album, Lovely, was released in 1988. Two more albums followed, Pure and Galore, before they disbanded.

John Coles described Crash simply as "classic." Sid Wilson thought they were a "quality band."

Bands like King and the Prims showed that Coventry's pool of talent was still expanding. Bands just kept on coming, creating new sounds for new audiences. Cov Aid came together for a good cause, showing not only that the city had a big heart but a very wide range of music to offer the world!

DOG & TRUMPET

60s/'70s Soul, RNB, Jazz

MOTOR CITY

DJs
Lof & Toby

AD-LIB
GREENS
TUESDAYS
8-11

LIVE
MUSIC
& DANCE
GUEST D.Js
PROGRAMME SEE OVER

jazz

jazz, latin and grooves
every thursday night 8.00 - 12.00
at the dog and trumpet

SAT ★ 4 ★ OCT
ROMA BAR • COVENTRY
RHYTHMDOC
PRESENTS
FROM LONDON TOWN.
THE TURNTABLE WIZ
KID B
KID B POSSE
BADDEST D.J. TO HIT TOWN
FUNK • SOUL • HOUSE
HIP HOP • REGGAE
8 TILL 12
£1.

DOG and TRUMPET
Friday 8-12
SILVERS
Saturday 8.30-12
BUSTERS
Tuesday 9-2

PRESENTED BY: JOHN COCA...

SOUL NIGHT
60s, 70s
MOTOWN STAX ATLANTIC
PHILLY NORTHERN MODERN
DOG + TRUMPET 8-11PM

A Certain Ratio
Entertain Live at...

FULL SUPPORTING RHYTHMIC MUSIC

DOCTOR LANG + A.C.R. D.J.

Guys Club 9pm-2am
Shelton sq. Coventry
WEDNESDAY FEBRUARY 17TH

THOSE HOT DJ NIGHTS! DANCING AT THE DOG, SILVERS AND STOKER

CHAPTER 10

One of many local bands in action at Stoker!

Was Coventry going to the dogs in the 1980s? No! But plenty of Dirty Stop Outs were going to the Dog, as the Dog and Trumpet was usually called, in search of great music and nights out.

For Gary Morton, it was a must-go-to place at the weekend.

"Many local bands played there which was great but also others before they became famous." He remembers Bad Manners gigging there before they hit the big time, as does Joe Reynolds, who was also present and correct that night!

Joe Reynolds "The Dog and Trumpet was a great venue in the early eighties for live music."

The pub's name came about because there was a cinema upstairs run by HMV. The logo for that company was a dog listening to the horn (trumpet) of an old fashioned gramophone. The owner of the underground music pub, music entrepreneur Ken Brown, thought it was a nice touch to call it that. The Dog was quite different to its previous incarnation as the Bier Keller with its 'oom-pah-pah,' Bavarian atmosphere.

From downstairs at the Dog music lovers might then head upstairs at the Silver Sword (or vice versa!) to the cracking music venue Silvers. The Dog and Silvers were central to a lot of what was happening in that era both in terms of live music and DJ nights. DJs such as Toby Davies, Paul Toller, Lof, Cap, John Cocaine and Rhythm Doctor Chris all gained huge followings due to the wide variety of music they played and their innovative styles. There was something for just about everyone, any night of the week!

IMPROVISATION CLUB

THURS ABOVE SILVER SWORD. DIG IT !

MILLENNIUM

Fridays upstairs at the SILVER SWORD
Trinity St. Coventry

HOUSE, RAP and beyond

DJs LOF (D&T Saturdays)
+ Down by law

FREE before 9pm then £1
Doors Close 11pm   12 o'clock BAR

THE REAL UNDERGROUND

● **HOORAY**
house and hip-hop
DJS LOF + TOBY • 50P BEFORE 10.00 THEN £1

● **SOUL**
60's, 70's and 80's
DJ TOBY • 50P BEFORE 10.00 THEN £1

● **JAZZ**
jazz, latin and grooves
DJ TOBY • 50P BEFORE 10.00 THEN £1

dog & trumpet

Rights of admission reserved
No admission after 11.00
All nights 12.00 bar

MILLENNIUM
the sound of the underground
DJs LOF + PAUL

HOUSE, RAP & BEYOND

S I L V E R S
UPSTAIRS AT THE SILVER SWORD
EVERY FRIDAY NIGHT • FREE BEFORE 9.00 THEN £1
NO ADMISSION AFTER 11.00 • 12.00 BAR

Alternative Night

CLASSIC, gOTHIC
tRASH & pUNK

PRESENTED BY
jOHN COCCAINE

dog & trumpet

50p before 10.00 then £1
No admission after 11.00 • 12.00 bar
Rights of admission reserved

FAT iNDIE NIGHT

iNDEPENDANT pOP
DJ CAP

S I L V E R S
UPSTAIRS AT THE SILVER SWORD
THURSDAY NIGHT • FREE BEFORE 9.00 THEN 50P

John Cocaine's
ALTERNATIVE MUSIC SHOW

Classic, Goth,
Trash & Punk

S I L V E R S
UPSTAIRS AT THE SILVER SWORD
EVERY SATURDAY • FREE BEFORE 9.00 THEN £1
NO ADMISSION AFTER 11.00 • 12.00 BAR

FRIDAYS
ALTERNATIVE
DJ
    J COCAINE

UPSTAIRS AT THE
SILVER SWORD FOR
6 WEEKS FROM 22/8/86
FREE BEFORE 9, 50p
9-10, 75p 10-11 DOORS
CLOSE. 12 BAR.

DANCE
DJs LOF + TOBY.
HOW COOL IS COOL'
SATURDAYS

Toby Davies: "In the early 1980s there was a very healthy scene of local bands at various venues across town on virtually any given night. The band scene shrunk, especially once Tiffany's closed, but had been great early on in the decade. The local DJs stepped in to fill the void."

They formed a collective and even produced a newsletter, called The Manual, full of news about gigs, bands and venues plus comment about the local music scene. And a bit of humour!

Toby Davies first tried his hand a DJing in the popular Downstairs Bar of the Lanch in 1979. He experienced such a thrill that night that he did it some more, then some more, at places like the Hope and Anchor pub and eventually the Dog and other city venues.

The thrill is still there and he's still DJing today. "I did, and still do, like to be in a busy dark room with people enjoying music."

Trev Teasdel heard about a new band in the making outside the Dog and Trumpet early in 1980 when he bumped into on old friend of his, Tony 'Mojo' Morgan.

"Tony told me he was starting new band called EMF – Electro Motive Force - and wanted to discuss my writing some songs for them. The concept of this new band would be ska mixed with a blues bass lines and sax. He later saw an ad in the local paper, two female singers with their own material wanting to form a band. Tony auditioned them and the band was then complete. They launched at the Dog and Trumpet.

A new 'Force' on the music front

Tony Mojo

Street Talk on the 2-Tone Revival

The Specials 10 years ago   Ranking Roger of The Beat   The Selecter back in 1979

Turning back the clock with 2-Tone

Spring beats late hitch to make club's launch

Show will go on as Vision helps out

THE MANUAL ISSUE ONE

a certain
architectu
Kahnwei
many a tr
distributio
parallel li
them into
printing t
drawn fla

But at
object—o
subordina
work mod
that can
between
is the art

Ten Classic Nights

Places Club Gauche was banned from... See above

H OORAY

DOG & TRUMPET
SATURDAYS
DEEP LATIN
HIP-HOP JAZZ
SOUL NEW-BEAT
DJ LOF

MASTERMIX

FAT THURSDAYS

Upstairs at the
SILVER SWORD
Trinity St, Coventry
FREE ENTRY
with this handout
any Thursday until Nov. 17th
before 10-30

MILLENNIUM
REFURBISHED AND VITAL

FRIDAYS
UPSTAIRS AT THE
SILVER SWORD
TRINITY ST, COVENTRY

HOUSE
RAP +
BEYOND

20 Evening Telegraph, Thursday, February 16, 1989

Alastair Law with the latest *Street Talk*

DJs club together to form a co-op

COVENTRY'S hottest record-spinners are pooling their talents to form the city's first DJ co-operative.

They want to put life and variety back into the Coventry nightclubbing scene.

DJs Lof, Toby and Cap are already well-known to dancers as the trio behind the turntables at The Silver Sword and The Dog And Trumpet.

Now they're injecting new blood into

Big in Texas: searching for a new drummer

their ranks and extending their repertoire to include all the latest sounds from house, rap and soul to indie, alternative, electronic body music and Belgian new beat.

DJs Russell and Matthew are the crew's latest additions.

The idea of forming a co-operative came from DJ Lof.

He told *Street Talk*: "The whole thing started with me a long time ago when I used to do discos at the Polytechnic.

"Cap and Toby used to come along and dance and asked me to play records.

"We got together and started doing discos as a trio and now we've taken on Russell and Matthew, who we met when they used to come and dance."

The new co-operative is now large enough to man four discos every week in Coventry, with a collection of records that runs into the thousands.

Tuesdays see Soul Night at The Dog And Trumpet with DJ Toby and on Thursdays there's a choice of Electronic Body Music at The Dog with DJ Russell or Indie Night with DJ Cap at The Silver Sword.

And Lof, Toby and Cap's Friday and Saturday spots are still big news with dancers from as far afield as Birmingham, Nottingham and Northampton travelling to Silvers and the Dog.

You can check the latest sounds being played in the top ten dance chart the trio compile each week for *Street Talk* (see below).

Toby said: "We won't make any profit in the co-operative. All the spare cash goes to buy records and some of them are very expen-

soul night
Dog + Trumpet

MOTOWN

STAX

ATLANTIC

all the best in
60's and 70's SOUL

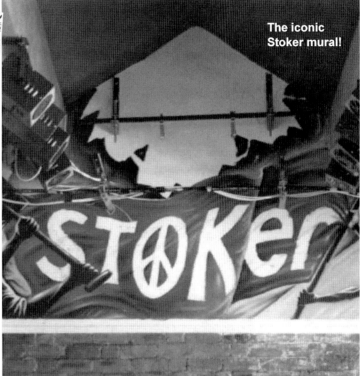

The iconic Stoker mural!

John Bradbury and myself helped the band load their equipment on the van afterwards."

The Rhythm Doctor was the resident DJ at the Dog and Trumpet from 1983, when local music promoter Ken Brown took over. He played a wide range of soul, ska, jazz, funk and reggae.

Chris had moved to Coventry in 1977 to study Fine Art at the Lanch, where many good things had come together music and entertainment-wise.

"The terrible prog rock freshers night pushed me over the edge to offer my services as a DJ there! It's still my profession 40 years on.

I was there at the birth of 2 Tone, being a good friend of Jerry Dammers since those days even before the Specials."

He began DJing in the Lanch's popular student's union bar, the Hope and Anchor plus other pubs. A man of many talents, Chris also worked with some of the lesser-known bands recording demos and mixing live sound. He was also a member of the Swinging Cats including when they supported the Specials on their final UK tour - 36 dates in 40 nights! DJ Chris took with him to the Dog and Trumpet loads of experience and fans.

Toby Davies remembers that Fridays at the Dog had a strong crowd with virtually everyone dressed in black.

"John Cocaine's thing was underground alternative rock music. Also very popular were the Groovy Garden nights on a Sunday."

Nigel Williams remembers those Sunday sessions well. He worked at the Wedge Café and was also in the Giraffes in the mid/late eighties. "I did the Groovy Garden disco on a Sunday night at

the Dog and Trumpet with the late Steve Edgson of the Giraffes, Reluctant Stereotypes and Pink Umbrellas."

The DJ sessions multiplied at the Dog, popular with the growing numbers of students in the city as well as Coventry's own music-loving youth.

75

Toby Davies: "By the last few months of 1989, the Dog had student parties virtually every Monday and Thursday. Tuesday was soul, Wednesday was indie and the weekends had three long established theme nights. I was fortunate enough to be playing Monday to Thursday and Saturday. Fridays was my official night off as Paul T would play Silvers but I'd often end up joining him."

Silvers ran an indie night on Thursdays. DJ Toby Davies says:

"This was a successful venture for 'DJ Cap', Tim Poulter, who was part of our loose collective of DJs from 1986-90. Originally known as 'Fat,' this ran well into the 1990s."

Also at the Silver Sword, roller skating DJ Jules Little and his mates used to relax after skating sessions at the Coventry Sports Centre. They

claimed to be 18 if anyone cared to ask.

One Friday evening in January 1987 turned out to be memorable.

"We were sat at the back of the Silver Sword when the DJ announced they had just got the late licence to open upstairs. 'Everybody, follow me, see you there in five minutes!' The room fell silent. The flock followed their musical shepherd to their new pasture upstairs. We didn't."

Feeling brave, he asked for the manager, telling him that anyone coming in would think it was pretty dead as there was no music. They wouldn't know about upstairs being open. He offered his own services. "I'm a DJ, I'll do it!"

He expected a few choice words and an ID check but instead the manager said he could start right there and then if he had Top 40 with him. He did, so off he went to spin some discs.

"What a break. My first paid DJ gig. £15 for the first two weeks as a trial." Jules went on to have a great DJing career.

Moving over to the Stoker

The Stoker was a bit out of town, on the Binley Road in Stoke, but drew in crowds from near and far.

In the late 1980s it became a popular community and arts centre, which included what Steve Ashwell describes as the "eponymous venue." He should know: he helped to set it up in the first place!

"It was a grand house, although much neglected. Little more than pile of bricks, really, but such an interesting space. It was an ideal spot being adjacent to the railway embankment that ran along Gosford Green, with remnants of ancient

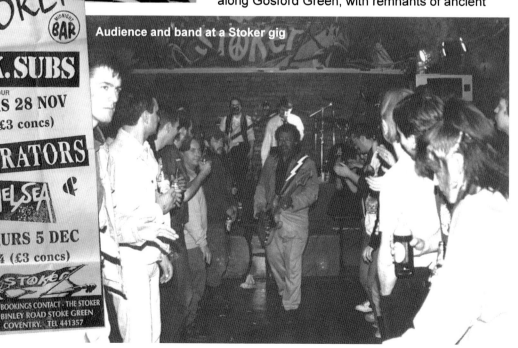

Audience and band at a Stoker gig

woodland and forgotten allotments at the back. A regular squat, with a tented encampment, and home to numerous anarchic activities over previous years, it seemed to us ripe for doing something positive with."

In 1986 the Stoke Green Community Association approached the city council for help in developing the site into a community-oriented facility. Through the Urban Programme, Steve was instrumental in getting some funding.

Basic refurbishments were carried out to secure and refit the building, which became the Stoke Green Community Centre. Steve says that it was "all very bingo and disco to start with!"

Further funding followed and the Stoke Musicians' Collective set about transforming the place into something viable, running all manner of projects there. This included the country's first Music Business and Technology course. Steve says:

"Many of Coventry's aspiring musicians passed through this course which not only gave them a professional qualification but kept them off the dole."

> **Steve Ashwell:** *"It took about two years to get the fully-equipped 200-capacity Stoker venue up and running. There was also a performance area outside which was the setting for bonfire extravaganzas, festivals and marquee events. There were   rehearsal, recording, arts and media facilities on-site, with environmental, sport and housing initiatives operating throughout the local area. It was a hive of activity and co-operatively run."*

The Stoker hosted plenty of gigs including the early Manics, pre-Oasis Oasis, Steve Marriott,

Albert Lee and many other punk, blues and jazz artists. Local bands played a major part in the Stoker's relatively short existence, 1988-91.

It attracted a variety of people including punks who weren't always welcome in more mainstream places according to Rich Mulligan. Leigh Torrance remembers The Stoker fondly as he played there a few times as did Richard King of the band Balloon Farm.

Time-limited from the outset, Stoker was bulldozed to make way for major road developments in that part of the city.

Back in the city, the West Indian Centre in Spon Street was another community-oriented venue that offered a variety of entertainment. In the late eighties it hosted the Democracy Club with local musicians performing such as Spring, as well as Coventry DJs Toby, Paul T and Lof.

A rather nomadic venue was the Tic Toc. It began life as a theatre group, the name itself standing for Theatre in Coventry, Theatre of Coventry. One claim to fame, according to Pete Clemons is that one of Coventry's very last gigs of the decade took place there.

"Late December 1989, the Giraffes played at the Tic Toc club."

By the end of the decade, Coventry's range of venues had shrunk, but smaller ones were doing their very best to keep people entertained. Places like the Stoker were short-lived, but made a big impact in their time.

The Tic Toc in Primrose Hill Street, late 1980s

COVENTRY CARNIVAL

SATURDAY JUNE 11th 1983

Number 3921

Official Programme

20p

Have fun while the old man goes to the dogs.

Bingo!

Above: A young Richard King - blue shirt and with corks dangling from his hat- in Sir Henry Parkes School's carnival float 1982

STOCK CAR RACING

BRISCA

COVENTRY STADIUM

• BRISCA Formula I •
The Mitchells & Butlers
BREW XI TROPHY
SATURDAY, 7th MAY, 1983 at 7.15 p.m.
Magazine Programme & Official Race Card 35 p

RAG '80
WARWICK UNIVERSITY & COVENTRY POLYTECHNIC

CINEMA, ALL THE FUN OF THE FAIR & CARNIVAL TIME!

No-one can hear you scream in outer space, or so we're told. But when a very nasty alien popped up at a dining table somewhere out there, screams were heard in Coventry's ABC cinema. It was January 1980 and Ridley Scott's Alien had just made its first appearance

The sight of this thing trying to gobble up Sigourney Weaver aka Ripley was the stuff of nightmares. Who could have guessed that Alien would be the first of many, with slobbering nasties still scaring us to bits years later?

Who could have guessed that Alien would be the first of many, with slobbering nasties still scaring us to bits years later?

In May 1980, we were whisked right out of our familiar universe with the release of the next instalment of Star Wars: The Empire Strikes Back. We loved it and helped to make it the highest grossing film of the year. Many Dirty Stop Outs queued round the block to see this, then waited patiently for the next installment, Return of the Jedi, in 1983.

Sarah Soden was amongst those early fans, seeing the first Star Wars at Theatre One in the summer of 1978 with her sister. She missed The Empire Strikes Back and made do with reading the paperback.

"I saw Return of the Jedi the night it was released, standing in line at the ABC cinema. I went again the next night. Before I saw the first one I had bought the Marvel comic, listened to the abridged radio play and devoured every article I could get my hands on. I was hyper-excited by the time I saw it, simply spellbound."

There's an interesting link between Coventry and the Star Wars films. A local DJ turned Professor in Sustainable Transport and Design was part of the team building an advanced version of R2-D2 for The Empire Strikes Back. Coventry's Lanchester Poly certainly has some famous alumni and Prof. John Jostins has to be added to that long list.

After graduating in 1978 he joined the team working on the new version of the loveable robotic companion to Hans Solo. A major detail to get right was making the model comfortable for actor Kenny

Baker who operated R2-D2. At one point a few household items were bought from Woolworths to help achieve that end!

Prof. Jostin continued to work on special effects including for Dr Who and Superman II. In an earlier incarnation he was a DJ with fellow Lanch Poly student Chris the Rhythm Doctor, who made quite a name for himself locally and further afield- Birmingham, London and Tallinn! DJ John Jostin was known to be very good on the decks as well but he chose a different but still very starry path!

And we were still floating around in outer space with the 11th James Bond film- Moonraker in 1980. Roger Moore was playing 007 for the fourth time and still clearly loving it.

There was a spacey feel to films at the start of the 1980s. People were perhaps feeling that things down here were looking a bit wobbly and another galaxy, far away, was an appealing prospect. But finding out that things up there were even worse, with evil empires, death stars, and slimy aliens, perhaps perked us up!

The popular TV series Star Trek went from the small to the big screen, with most of the TV cast starring in their usual roles. There was a comforting familiarity seeing Leonard Nimoy as Spock and William Shatner at the Enterprise's helm as Captain Kirk.

Series creator Gene Roddenberry was instrumental in getting the series to cinema audiences. Once again few could have guessed that, like the TV series, the films would run and run becoming what we now recognize as a film franchise.

And then came the iconic Bladerunner in 1983 also directed by Ridley Scott and with Harrison Ford starring as

Rick Deckard. The action all took place on a very dark and dismal looking future earth where people were promised a better life on the "off-world" by constant bombardment of neon lit adverts. We never did see that "off-world!"

All the fun of the fair and carnival time!

People realized that the chance of zooming around the universe anytime soon was zero but they could take a more sedate ride on a flying machine at the fair.

Twice a year, a fair appeared on Hearsall Common as it had done for decades. It was very much part of the Dirty Stop Outs annual routine. It was a place for a bit of escapism, with thrills and spills galore until your spending money ran out! The same stallholders came most years. Some of them took on local lads to help erect the rides and work on them for a few hours.

There were the dodgems, waltzers and big wheel, all "brilliant rides" in Sue Lowe's view and extra thrilling when all lit up at night.

Food-wise, there was plenty on offer, if you had the stomach for it either before or after being shook up and spun round on the various rides.

Sue Lowe says the food smells were "unforgettable- pungent and greasy." There was candy floss, toffee apples, hot dogs and burgers with fried onions, ketchup and mustard.

"We used to eat with our fingers, as we wandered around the stalls and rides, catching sight of the poor gold fish as they lingered in their plastic bags."

Being a dog lover, Sue remembers the old man who ran the rifle range who had a tiny grey poodle that sat patiently in its small basket as the air rifles were loaded.

The 'crock fair' also came every year, usually around Whitsun. There was entertainment to be had as well as cheap crockery as many stallholders used to throw up in the air wicker baskets with entire dinner services in them! They knew how to do that without breaking a single plate. It was always thrilling to watch.

The banter was also part of the fun with audiences trying to bag a bargain. Anything from casserole dishes, saucepans to coffee mugs and towels could be found at the crock fair.

Also very down to earth and good fun for participants and spectators alike was the Coventry Carnival. It was one of the biggest public events of the year, usually in June, involving people of all ages. Many Dirty Stop Outs grew up with the carnival as an annual treat and some participated on the floats that made up the procession.

It was about the community coming together to raise money for charity as well as about providing an entertaining spectacle.

Liz Smith loved the carnival.

"Me and my mum would go into town and find a good spot in Trinity Street. All the littlies would sit

'Captain' Paul Michael Kennelly and the Iron Brigade boys, with decked out Land Rover ready for Coventry Carnival June 1982

The Iron Brigade of the American Civil War society in Coventry Carnival June 1982, Warwick Rd

on the edge of the road with the crowd would be four or five deep behind us. We'd chatter excitedly and then stop, straining for those first sounds, usually the tinkling of the percussion bells, then the drum, the deep base first, sounding the beat, then the others, until you could hear the full band as they drew nearer!"

At this point, many people would jump up and start waving their flags and get prepared to throw their small change into the collecting buckets of the people on or walking alongside the floats.

> *Liz Smith "Some years there seemed to be hundreds of floats in the carnival and it would go on forever!"*

As a youngster, Richard King had the pleasure of being on his school's float participating in the 1982 carnival. Dressed in a blue shirt, a hat with corks dangling around it and red Kickers, he was part of his school's float. But why the Australian-style fancy dress?

His school in Canley was named after a local man who became a famous politician 'down under'- Sir Henry Parkes. Referred to as the father of the Australian Federation, Sir Henry had very humble beginnings, born in 1815 to a very poor tenant farmer in the Canley area. After emigrating to Australia, he was able to educate himself and rise to the status of a respected politician, doing much good work along the way.

There was even a statue of a kangaroo outside Sir Henry Parkes school, where Richard's mum was school secretary for many years and helped organise the carnival float.

From Australia to America - Coventry carnival floats and bands were inspired by themes from around the world. As captain of the Iron Brigade American Civil War society, Paul Michael Kennelly took part in 1982's carnival on June 13th. The Brigade proudly waved their flags as they marched alongside a suitably decorated Land Rover.

Many of Coventry's factories and firms organised floats for the carnival, with employees happily getting on board, literally, and donning fancy dress for the day. It was good fun and probably what would now be called a good 'team building' exercise!

A Carnival Queen's story

For Tracey McAtamney, 1985 was very special indeed - she had been crowned Carnival Queen! Her journey began when her mum Shirley entered her for the competition. "I didn't know she'd done that! I had just started work at a solicitor's office on Ball Hill. I loved my job and everyone was really supportive when I was shortlisted as a finalist."

The interviews took place in the Council House with the Lord Mayor Councillor Bill McKernan part of the judging panel. Tracey was asked about her work and hobbies.

"At the time I was a venture scout and was involved in raising money for various charities." That answer was helpful as the carnival was very much about charity.

The night came when the Carnival Queen would be crowned at the Lord Mayor's Ball at the De Vere Hotel, a formal black-tie event. Tracey felt like a princess in her white cocktail dress. "All the family attended including my Granddad Cyril, who was so proud."

The evening began with a champagne reception followed by a three-course meal but Tracey was too nervous to eat a thing!

Mercia Sound presenter Stuart Linell was the host for the evening and he spoke to each of the five finalists.

"When it was my turn to speak I was asked about the venture scouts. I made everyone laugh because I explained although I loved the outdoors, I was not that great at it. On one occasion I returned dressed in bin liners having fallen in the mud.

"I remember holding my breath when the winners were announced in reverse. Hayley was called third, followed by Michelle second and then I was announced as the winner. A bright red cape was wrapped around me together with a beautiful crown. The rest of the evening was a blur of laughter, music and dancing.

"I can remember being woken by the home phone at 8.00am on a Sunday morning. Photographers from the Coventry Evening Telegraph and the Citizen were being sent to interview me. This was the start of an amazing year!"

Carnival day arrived in June along with very hot weather.

"Michelle, Hayley and I were all treated like royalty. We had our hair and makeup professionally done and we each had a stunning dress designed for us. We certainly did feel special being picked up by the Lord Mayor's car, COV 1."

After a formal lunch at Coventry's Guild Hall, they were taken to the Memorial Park where the fairground was in full swing.

"We joined the procession and had a day to remember leading the procession through the streets of Coventry. I felt so honoured!"

Over the course of her Carnival Queen year, Tracey fulfilled many duties including opening around 30 summer fayes. She sometimes had two invitations in one day but enjoyed them all and was always treated as a VIP.

Tracey took part in opening Coventry Swimming Baths and Motor Museum. Along with the Lady Mayoress Ann McKernan, chauffeur Mary Rutter and Michelle they did a 2000 foot parachute jump!

"It was incredible! We eventually completed our jump after many hours of training and two cancellations due to weather conditions. We raised in excess of £26,000 which was split between two local charities."

Throughout the year Tracey was also was instrumental in the launch of the Coventry Evening Telegraph's Snowball Appeal and was crowned Miss Coventry City, at the city football ground.

The 1980s may have seen visions of the future and outer space at Coventry cinemas, but the annual fair remained very popular as did the carnival which was also an important community and charity-oriented event.

Tracey McAtamney crowned Carnival Queen for 1985!

Inset: Queen for a year! Carnival Queen Tracey

ACKNOWLEDGEMENTS

Pete Chambers, BEM, music writer, director and curator of Coventry's Music Museum plus Museum team; Pete Clemons, local music writer; staff at the Herbert's Local History Centre and the Modern Records Library, Warwick University; DJ Toby Davies, DJ 'Rhythm Doc' Chris Long; musician/music producer Martin Bowes; DJ Rich Mulligan; photographers Bill Boswell and Robin Brooker.

To all the members of the Dirty Stop Outs Facebook group who have shared memories, stories and photos. A huge thanks for their enduring support and humour. Tina Folan and the Coventry Old and New Facebook group; Rob Orland and the Historic Coventry Forum.

For additional materials and information: Steve Ashwell, Nick Edgington, Luke Garland, David Gilbert, Pete Hill, Col Hughes, Linda Keller, Mike Lewis, DJ Jules Little; Sue Long, Sue Lowe, Tracey McAtamney, Paul Michael Kennelly, Anne Porter, Philip Sephton, Maxine Smyth, Trev Teasdel, Bob Waggitt, Alan West.

THE AUTHOR

Ruth Cherrington grew up in a Coventry suburb but soon headed for the city's bright lights and nightlife. With a social club right across the street from her home, Ruth was a young Dirty Stop Out and gained a Degree in Having a Good Time long before a BA and MA in Sociology. She was a lecturer for over 25 years and travelled the world for work and wonderful times. Ruth put her experiences of the local club at the centre of her book Not Just Beer and Bingo! (Authorhouse 2012.) She also set-up the Club Historians website- www.clubhistorians.co.uk. She has written articles and blogs on Coventry social history and culture and is no stranger to TV and radio. Last year she wrote the best-selling Dirty Stop Out's Guide to 1970s Coventry.

Ruth at Pool Meadow bus station, going somewhere, again!

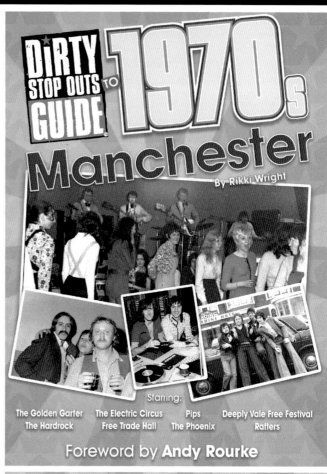
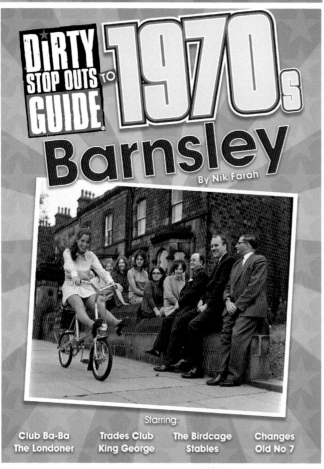
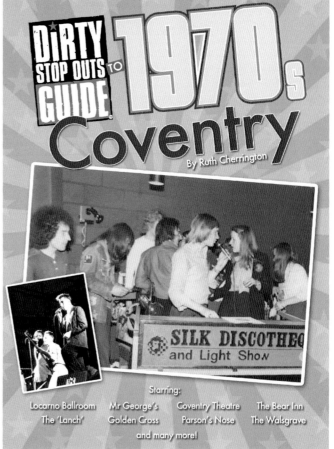